PARTY CROCHET

PARTY CROCHET

SUE WHITING

NEW
HOLLAND

This paperback edition first published in 2008 by
New Holland Publishers (UK) Ltd
London • Cape Town • Sydney • Auckland

Garfield House, 86–88 Edgware Road
London W2 2EA
www.newhollandpublishers.com

80 McKenzie Street, Cape Town 8001 South Africa

Unit 1, 66 Gibbes Street, Chatswood, NSW 2067, Australia

218 Lake Road, Northcote, Auckland, New Zealand

ISBN   978 1 84773 223 1

Senior editor: Corinne Masciocchi
Pattern checker: Sue Horan
Artworks: Ben Cracknell, Carrie Hill and Kuo Kang Chen
Photography: Sian Irvine
Cover Photography: Damian Sandone
Designer: Isobel Gillan
Production: Hazel Kirkman
Editorial direction: Rosemary Wilkinson

10 9 8 7 6 5 4 3 2 1

Reproduction by Pica Digital PTE Ltd, Singapore
Printed and bound by Times Offset, Malaysia

Contents

Introduction

Luscious lurex, mouth-watering mohair, cuddly chenille, romantic ribbons and sparkling speciality yarns are easily transformed into perfect party wear with a little help from a crochet hook!

Crochet is easy – take a ball of yarn, a crochet hook and a little inspiration and you are ready to go. And here you should find more than enough inspiration to help you create that perfect party outfit – with surprisingly little effort. Whether you are looking for glamorous and elegant evening wear or a funky little number to pop on with jeans and a T shirt to visit friends, there's something here for everyone. It doesn't matter if you are a total novice crocheter or not, that shouldn't stop you – there's just as many quick and easy makes here as there are projects that might challenge you!

Crochet is growing in popularity – both as a craft and as a fashion statement. Nearly every big name now includes a little crochet somewhere in their collection – from high street stores to the biggest couture houses. And now you can be up there too. Once you've got the hang of the few basic stitches you are ready to start to create your very own 'designer original'.

Almost all the hand knitting yarns that are available now in yarn stores can be used for crochet – and here you'll find some of the best and most exciting yarns around turned into stunning garments you'll love to wear.

With crochet, there's only ever one stitch on your hook at any time so there's very little chance of dropping stitches and making mistakes. All the different crochet stitches are based on one simple principle – insert the hook into the work, wrap the yarn around the hook and pull a loop through. That's all there is to it! It's just the way the hook is inserted and how the yarn is wrapped around it that creates the stunning effects it's easy to achieve in crochet. And here you'll find all the techniques you need to help you on your way as well as the patterns you'll need to create your very own masterpiece.

And why not try adding beads and sequins to your crochet to add even more impact? Here there's lots of designs to make that use these to great effect, whether you want to just add a few beads to try a new technique or masses of sequins to make a dramatic statement. And the selection of beads and sequins around is vast too – from subtle seed beads to glamorous crystals, from pearls to paillette sequins. So long as you can thread it onto your yarn, you can use it!

Crochet is fun – so it's the ideal way to make fun party wear. So what's stopping you? Start flicking through now, choose your design and get the party started!

Basic Information

WHAT YOU WILL NEED

All that is really needed to crochet an item is a crochet hook, some yarn and a pattern.

Crochet hooks

Crochet hooks, like knitting needles, come in lots of different sizes and are often made of different materials. Larger hooks are usually plastic but it is possible to buy ones made from bamboo – many people find this type particularly easy and comfortable to work with. Smaller hooks are usually metal, although some may consist of a metal hook and shank encased in a plastic handle.

The size of the hook used determines the size of the stitches being made, and it is also usually governed by the thickness of the yarn. Thick yarns are usually worked using a chunky hook, whilst fine yarns generally require a small hook.

Nowadays crochet hook sizes are generally given in a metric size – but if you have old hooks, carrying an older imperial measurement, you need to know what the metric equivalent is.

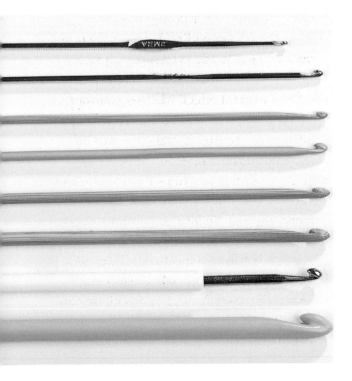

Crochet hook conversion chart

Metric	Old UK	USA
2.00 mm	14	B1
2.25 mm	13	B1
2.50 mm	12	C2
3.00 mm	11	D3
3.25 mm	10	D3
3.50 mm	9	E4
3.75 mm	–	F5
4.00 mm	8	G6
4.50 mm	7	7
5.00 mm	6	H8
5.50 mm	5	I9
6.00 mm	4	J10
6.50 mm	3	K10$^1/_2$
7.00 mm	2	–
8.00 mm	0	L11
9.00 mm	00	M13
10.00 mm	000	N15

- If more than one hook size is used for the item, it is important to adjust the size of these other hooks accordingly too.
- When making the slip knot, ensure that the end of the yarn that tightens the loop is the cut end of yarn, not the end leading to the ball – this will mean that the slip knot can be pulled up tighter later to neaten the work.
- When working any crochet stitch, the yarn should always be wrapped around the hook in the same way – over, round and under.

Yarns

Almost any yarn sold for hand knitting can be used for crochet – but some are easier to use than others! Beginners will find smooth yarns far easier to work with than textured ones. A fancy yarn that has a fluffy or boucle surface can easily catch on the crochet hook, making it difficult to pull the yarn through when working the stitches, and tricky to find exactly where to insert the hook.

The yarns used in this book are varied – some are fine smooth yarns, either plain or sparkly, and some are heavily textured – but all are ideally suited to making stylish party wear.

- **Colinette Giotto** 50% cotton, 40% rayon, 10% nylon, 144 m/157^1/$_2$ yds per 100 g (3^1/$_2$ oz) hank.
- **Lion Brand Incredible** 100% nylon, 100 m /110 yds per 50 g (1^3/$_4$ oz) ball.
- **Rowan Cotton Glace** 100% cotton, 115 m /137 yds per 50 g (1^3/$_4$ oz) ball.
- **Rowan Kidsilk Haze** 70% super kid mohair, 30% silk, 210 m/229 yds per 25 g (1 oz) ball.
- **Rowan Kidsilk Night** 67% super kid mohair, 18% silk, 10% polyester, 5% nylon, 208 m/227 yds per 25 g (1 oz) ball.
- **Rowan Lurex Shimmer** 80% viscose, 20% polyester, 95 m/104 yds per 25 g (1 oz) ball.
- **Rowan RYC Soft Lux** 64% extra fine merino wool, 10% angora, 24% nylon, 2% metallic fibre, 125 m/137 yds per 50 g (1^3/$_4$ oz) ball.
- **Sirdar Frenzy** 66% polyester, 34% nylon, 43 m/47 yds per 50 g (1^3/$_4$ oz) ball.
- **Sirdar Wow!** 100% polyester, 58 m/63^1/$_2$ yds per 100 g (3^1/$_2$ oz) ball.
- **Twilleys Goldfingering** 80% viscose, 20% metallised polyester, 200 m/219 yds per 50 g (1^3/$_4$ oz) ball.
- **Twilleys Silky** 100% viscose, 200 m/219 yds per 50 g (1^3/$_4$ oz) ball.
- **Wendy Chic** 60% nylon, 30% polyester, 10% metallised polyester, 80 m/87^1/$_2$ yds per 50 g (1^3/$_4$ oz) ball.

Extras

Apart from the yarn, hook and pattern there are very few extra items needed to complete a crochet project. Scissors will be needed to cut the yarn, and a tape measure is required to check the tension and that the work is the correct length. A blunt-pointed sewing needle – like the sort used for cross stitch or tapestry – will be needed to sew up the pieces. Everything else that may be required – such as beads or buttons – will be detailed with the pattern instructions.

THE IMPORTANCE OF TENSION

If many hours are to be spent making a crochet item, it's a good idea to make sure it's going to be the correct size! It is vitally important to the success of a project that the tension achieved matches that stated within the pattern, as the tension governs the final size of the crocheted pieces. If the tension is not correct, not only will the pieces not fit together as they should, but the finished item will not be the correct size and it may also mean that extra yarn will be required, or some may be left over.

Checking the tension

Before beginning the actual item, a tension swatch should be worked. Crochet has a tendency to pull in slightly as the work grows so this tension swatch must be quite large – ideally 15 cm (6 in) square. Work this tension swatch in the stitch pattern given within the "Tension" section and using the hook size stated and the correct yarn. Once the swatch is complete, lay it flat and mark out 10 cm (4 in) both across and along the rows with pins.

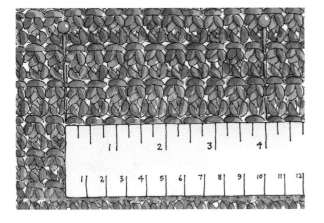

Count the number of stitches and rows (or pattern repeats if this is how the tension is given) between these marked points and check it matches the tension stated on the pattern. If there are more stitches or rows than stated within the pattern, the work is too tight and another swatch should be worked using a size larger hook. If there are too few stitches or rows, the work is too loose and a smaller size hook will be needed. Once the correct tension has been obtained, the size of hook required to achieve this tension is the size that should be used for the item.

THE BASIC STITCHES

Crochet is very simple as it basically consists of just a few different stitches, all of which are worked in a very similar way – it is their heights that vary. There is only ever one stitch on the hook at any one time and the new stitches are worked by inserting the hook through the work, wrapping the yarn round the hook and pulling these loops of yarn through the stitch on the hook.

Slip knot

To start the work there needs to be the first original stitch on the hook! This is formed by making a slip knot and slipping this knot over the hook.

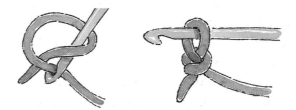

Make the slip knot by forming the yarn end into a loop. Insert the hook through this loop and pull another loop of yarn through the first loop. Gently pull on the yarn end to tighten this second loop around the body of the hook and the first stitch has been created.

Chain stitch

This is the basic starting point for almost all crochet projects.

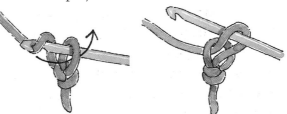

To make a chain stitch, wind the yarn around the hook by passing it over, round and under the hook. Now gently ease this new loop of yarn through the loop on the hook to complete the chain stitch.

Slip stitch

A slip stitch adds virtually no extra height to the work and is often used to join stitches together.

To work a slip stitch, insert the hook into the work as detailed in the pattern and take the yarn around the hook in the same way as for a chain stitch. Now bring this new loop of yarn through both the work and the stitch on the hook.

Double crochet

One of the most basic and frequently used crochet stitches, a double crochet is a short neat stitch.

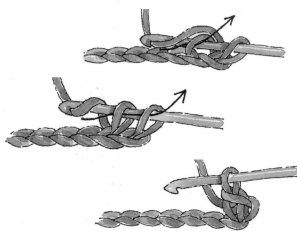

Start the double crochet stitch by inserting the hook into the work, taking the yarn around the hook and pulling this new loop of yarn through the work – there are now 2 loops of yarn on the hook. Take the yarn round the hook again and bring this new loop of yarn through both the loops on the hook to complete the stitch.

Treble

Another commonly used crochet stitch is the treble stitch – quite a tall, upright stitch.

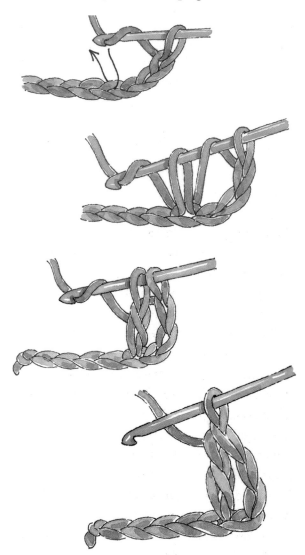

Make a treble by wrapping the yarn around the hook before inserting it into the work. Insert the hook into the work and wrap the yarn around the hook again. Bring this loop of yarn through the work so that there are 3 loops of yarn on the hook. Wrap the yarn around the hook and pull this new loop through just 2 of the loops on the hook – there are now 2 loops on the hook. Again, wrap the yarn around the hook and pull this loop through both the loops already on the hook to finish the stitch.

■ Taller treble-like stitches can be made in exactly the same way as double and triple trebles – check the pattern abbreviations to find out how many times the yarn should be wrapped around the hook for the type of stitch being worked.

■ Leave quite a long end before the initial slip knot and when fastening off so that this length of yarn can be used to sew up the seams, avoiding the need to join in more lengths of yarn.

■ If you are unsure as to what size to make, measure a similar garment from your wardrobe and make the size garment that has this "actual size" stated.

■ When working into a chain stitch, it is easier and neater to insert the hook between the 2 strands making up the "V" of the chain – but remember to also pick up the strand lying underneath these 2 strands, so that 2 of the 3 strands that form the chain are enclosed in the new stitch.

Treble variations

A treble stitch is created by wrapping the yarn around the hook once before inserting it into the work, drawing through a new loop and then pulling more loops of yarn through pairs of loops on the hook to complete the stitch. Taller treble-like stitches can be created by wrapping the yarn around the hook more times before it is inserted into the work.

To make a **double treble**, wrap the yarn around the hook twice before inserting it into the work. Wrap the yarn round the hook and draw the new loop through the work, leaving 4 loops on the yarn. Wrap the yarn around the hook again and pull this loop through 2 of the 4 loops on the hook – 3 loops now on the hook. Continue wrapping the yarn around the hook and bringing this new loop through pairs of loops already on the hook until there is just one loop left on the hook. For a double treble, this will be done a total of 3 times.

To make a **triple treble** stitch, wrap the yarn round the hook 3 times before inserting it and repeat the (yarn around hook and draw new loop through 2 existing loops) process a total of 4 times. Similarly, to make a **quadruple treble**, wrap the yarn around the hook 4 times before it is inserted into the work and repeat the (yarn around hook and draw new loop through 2 existing loops) process a total of 5 times.

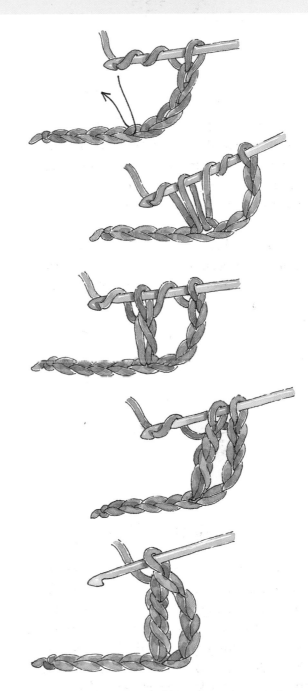

- It's a good idea to collect together everything you need for your item before you begin so that it is to hand whilst working.
- It is essential to check your crochet tension for every item made. Whilst you may achieve the tension stated with the hook stated on a dense crochet fabric, if the design uses a lot of lacy or chain stitches you may need to adjust your hook size as almost every crocheter will work tall stitches and chains at a different tension.

- Make sure you read through the explanation of any special abbreviation before starting to work so that you fully understand how to construct this special stitch, or stitch group.
- Many crocheters find it easier to follow a pattern by circling the figures that relate to the size they are making before starting. To avoid permanently marking the pattern, circle these figures in pencil so that these markings can be rubbed out later.

Half treble

This stitch is a combination of a double crochet and a treble stitch and makes a stitch roughly midway between these two in height.

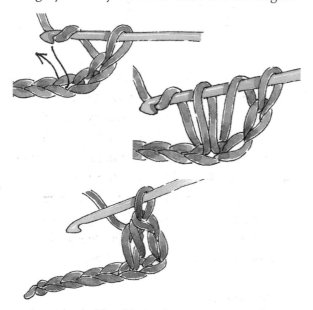

Start the half treble in the same way as for a treble – wrap the yarn around the hook and insert the hook into the work. Take the yarn around the hook and draw this new loop through the work so that there are 3 loops on the hook. Now complete the half treble as though it were a double crochet stitch by wrapping the yarn around the hook again and drawing this new loop through **all** the loops on the hook.

PLACING THE STITCHES

Varying effects can be created with the same basic crochet stitch by inserting the hook through the work in different ways.

Through the top of a stitch

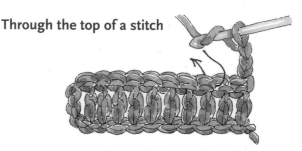

This is the most common placement for the new stitch and is the way the hook should be inserted into the work unless the pattern states otherwise. Across the top of stitches there will nearly always be a "V" shape formed by 2 strands of yarn. Insert the hook through the work, from front to back, under both of these strands to make the new stitch.

Through one loop only

Special effects can be created on the surface of the work by just picking up one of the 2 strands that form the "V" sitting on top of a stitch when working the new one. Check the pattern to see which of the 2 strands it should be, and insert the hook under this strand only, inserting it from front to back, instead of under both. If all the strands along one side of the previous row are left unworked, a "bar" of yarn will be left sitting across the work and the work will have a tendency to fold along this line.

Between the stitches

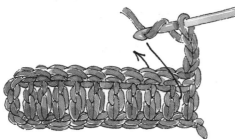

Inserting the hook between 2 stitches will create a fabric that is a little more open than if the stitches were placed on top of the previous ones. But, if the yarn is heavily textured, it will be much easier to work out exactly where to insert the hook! To work a stitch placed in this way, simply slide the hook through the work, from front to back, between the 2 stitches specified in the pattern.

Into chain spaces

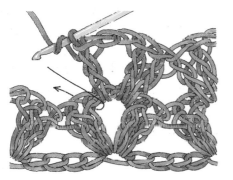

Lacy stitch patterns and motifs often place stitches into a "hole", or chain space, created in the work. When working into a chain space, insert the hook through this "hole", from front to back, and work the stitch so that the entire chain is enclosed by the new stitch.

CREATING A FABRIC

Strings of crochet stitches need to be placed one on top of the other in order to create a fabric, and these strings can either be worked backwards and forwards in rows, or round and round to form rounds.

Turning chains

However the stitches are positioned to form the fabric, the working loop used for the new stitches is generally on the top of a stitch. So, at the end of one row or round, this working loop nccds to be raised up to the top of the stitches that will form the new row or round – and this is done by working a few chain stitches, known as a "turning chain".

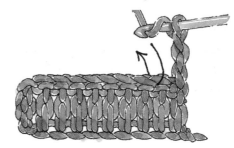

The number of chain stitches that need to be worked will vary according to the type of stitches being worked – for example, a treble stitch is roughly equal in height to 3 chain stitches, but a double crochet to just one chain stitch. Throughout this book, the pattern states exactly what is needed to be worked at the beginning and end of each row or round to bring the working loop to the required position for the next set of stitches.

Working in rows

The simplest way to form a crochet fabric is by working backwards and forwards in rows of stitches, with a turning chain at the beginning of each row. The work should be turned at the end of each row, working one row with the right side of the work facing and the following row with the wrong side of the work facing.

Working in rounds

Crochet can also be worked to form circular tubes of crochet, starting with a length of chain that is joined to form a loop, or flat disks, formed by ever-growing rounds worked into a tiny ring of chain stitches.

Each round of crochet is worked in a similar way to a row but the ends of the rounds are joined, usually by working a slip stitch into the top of the first stitch. Crochet stitches appear different when viewed from the right side to when viewed from the wrong side, so it is advisable to check whether the pattern being followed requires the work to be turned or not at the end of each round. If the item being crocheted combines sections worked in rounds and rows, it is advisable to turn the work at the end of each round to create a fabric that looks the same as when worked in rows.

Fastening off
Once each crochet section has been completed there will still be one stitch on the hook. This stitch should be fastened off by cutting the yarn and drawing this yarn end through the final stitch. Pull gently on the end to secure it.

FOLLOWING A CROCHET PATTERN
A crochet pattern should give all the information needed to make the item. Before beginning it is a good idea to read through the whole pattern to understand exactly how the item will be constructed.

Measurements
This section gives details of what size the item will be when completed and, in the case of a garment, what size body it should fit. Garments normally have a little "ease" added and will measure more than the body they are designed to fit.

Materials
This section of the pattern will list everything needed to make the item – the amount and type of yarn required, the size of crochet hook to use and anything else that may be needed to complete the item, such as beads or buttons.

The amounts of yarn stated are based on average requirements and are therefore approximate. If a garment is lengthened or shortened more or less yarn will needed. Even with modern technology, batches of yarn dyed at separate times can vary very slightly in colour and, whilst not apparent in the ball, this variation can often become very clear once the item is made. It is therefore advisable to buy all the yarn needed to complete the item at the same time, ensuring each ball carries the same "dye lot" number.

Abbreviations
Crochet uses a "shorthand" system to save writing out in full each and every stitch to be worked, abbreviating each stitch type down to just a few letters. Many abbreviations are common to all crochet patterns and these frequently-used abbreviations are all listed opposite. Sometimes a pattern will use a stitch that is specific to just this one design and a special abbreviation will be given.

Tension
The tension section of the design gives the details of the tension needed to recreate the item photographed. Sometimes the tension and the hook size specified will be different than expected for that type of yarn in order to create a particular effect for that item.

Making the item
Many crochet patterns are given in more than one size. The amount of stitches or measurements needed for each size are given as strings of numbers in round brackets ( ). If the second size is being made, then the second set of figures should be used whenever the bracketed figures appear.

If only one number is given, then it should be followed for all sizes. This happens in projects where the exact finished size of the

ABBREVIATIONS

beaded ch – slide bead up next to work, yoh and draw loop through leaving bead sitting against RS of work

beaded dc – insert hook as indicated, slide bead up next to work, yoh and draw loop through leaving bead sitting against RS of work, yoh and draw through both loops on hook

sequined dc – insert hook as indicated, slide sequin up next to work, yoh and draw loop through leaving sequin sitting against RS of work, yoh and draw through both loops on hook

alt	alternate	mm	millimetres
beg	beginning	patt	pattern
ch	chain	rem	remaining
cm	centimetres	rep(s)	repeat(s)
cont	continue	RS	right side
dc	double crochet	sp(s)	space(s)
dec	decreas(e)(ing)	ss	slip stitch
dtr	double treble	st(s)	stitch(es)
foll	following	tr(s)	treble(s)
htr	half treble	WS	wrong side
in	inches	yoh	yarn over hook
inc	increas(e)(ing)		

item being made is not crucial, as with the various accessories featured in the book.

When more than one stitch is to be worked into an area, this group of stitches is also shown in round brackets ( ) as a series of stitches. All the stitches in the round brackets should be worked into the place stated after the brackets.

Occasionally a pattern will require a certain group of stitches to be repeated more than once; this group is shown in square brackets [ ]. The instructions contained in these square brackets should be repeated the number of times stated after the closing bracket.

Crochet stitch patterns often require the same group of stitches to be repeated many times across a row or round. A star * appears at the beginning of the section to be repeated. Return to the star to begin the next repeat.

Occasionally there will also be a double star ** appearing within a starred section of repeats. The pattern will state that the last repeat of the section should end at this point, ignoring the remaining instructions that were repeated previously. Instructions will then be given for what to do next.

Most crochet items are made in more than one piece; it's a good idea to make these sections in the order stated on the pattern otherwise it may be difficult to complete the garment as the pieces often refer back to previous sections for certain measurements, or require pieces to be complete in order to add another piece.

Once all sections have been made, the written pattern tells how to join the sections to complete the item. It also gives instructions for any edgings or trims to be added. Once again, it is important to follow the order of making up and joining the pieces so that any extra sections, such as collars, cuffs and bands can be worked along the correct edges.

Following crochet diagrams

The stitch pattern used for a crochet item can be shown on a diagram. This diagram provides a visual reference of exactly how the stitches that make up the pattern fit together. The diagram uses a different symbol for each type of stitch worked, using tall symbols for tall stitches and short symbols for short stitches, with these symbols being placed together as they would be on the finished work. As with abbreviations, certain symbols are common to many crochet patterns whilst some symbols are specific to one particular stitch pattern. Each diagram should be accompanied by a key explaining what each symbol means.

O : ch
● : ss
+ : dc
⊤ : htr
⫪ :tr
⫪ : dtr

■ Sometimes the beads will "move" through the crochet fabric as further rows or rounds are added and you may need to gently ease them back through to the right side of the work once the crochet section has been completed.

■ Each motif is generally made in the same way as every other motif – but it is a good idea to double check on the pattern that this is the case!

■ Be careful when placing the first and last stitches of rows of crochet that these are worked into the correct place. If the turning chain is counted as the first stitch of this new row, do NOT work into the stitch at the base of this chain. And, at the ends of rows, make sure to place the last stitch in the top of the turning chain of the previous row if this chain replaced the first stitch.

■ Take care not to twist the base chain when joining the ends to form the foundation ring as this can make the edge uneven and spoil the work.

SHAPING WITHIN CROCHET

Not all crochet items are made from simple tubes or strips of crochet, and stitches will need to be increased or decreased to create the final pieces. The pattern instructions will normally set out exactly what combination of stitches need to be worked to achieve this shaping whilst still retaining the stitch pattern.

Decreasing is often achieved in crochet by working two stitches so that they join at the top, forming an upside-down V shape. Each stitch, or 'leg', forming this V shape is worked in the normal way up to the last stage. Once both stiches have been worked to this point, the individual stiches, or 'legs', are joined by taking the yarn over the hook and drawing this new loop of yarn through all the loops on the hook, thereby joining the two stiches at the top.

WORKING WITH BEADS AND SEQUINS

Many of the items in this book use beads or sequins to create the finished effect, and these are attached whilst the item is being crocheted.

Using beads

When working with beads, these need to be threaded onto the yarn before starting to crochet the pieces. To thread the beads onto the yarn, start by threading a sewing needle with sewing thread, making sure the chosen needle used will easily pass through the beads! Knot the thread ends, to form a loop of sewing

thread, and slip the cut end of the yarn through this loop. Thread a bead onto the needle, and then gently slide it along the sewing thread and onto the yarn. Continue in this way until the required number of beads are on the yarn.

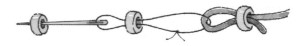

As the crochet is worked, the beads on the yarn should be moved along the yarn away from the work until they are needed. However, as repeatedly sliding many beads along a delicate yarn can damage the yarn, it is a good idea to thread the beads on in groups of no more than about 200–300 at a time. Once these beads have been used, break the yarn, thread on the same number again and re-join the yarn.

To work a beaded crochet stitch – either a double crochet or a chain stitch – start by sliding a bead up along the yarn so that it sits right next to the last stitch worked. Insert the hook and make the next stitch in the normal way, leaving the bead sitting at the back of the work.

When shaping the edges (such as for an armhole or neck) of a beaded section, take care not to place a bead on the end stitch of a row as this could make it difficult to attach this section to any other section it needs to be seamed to later.

Using sequins

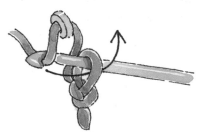

Sequins can be threaded onto the crochet yarn in exactly the same way as beads. However, as the holes in sequins are often larger than those in beads, it is sometimes possible to simply thread them straight onto the yarn.

Sequinned double crochet and chain stitches are worked in exactly the same way as beaded stitches. Sequins can, however, sometimes fold themselves up the wrong way as they are attached and it may be necessary, once the section is complete, to just gently smooth the sequins down so that they all lie in the same direction.

MOTIFS

Some of the designs in this book are made up of lots of small motifs that are joined together to form the finished item and there is often a diagram that will show how these motifs are to be joined.

When working a motif, the tension section will often state the size one finished motif should be, as it is not possible to give a stitch and row tension. It is vitally important this motif size is matched exactly if the item is to fit.

Where an item is made up of motifs, the pattern instructions will normally state what shape one motif should be when completed, and give details of what there is around the outer edge of this first motif. Once the first motif has been worked, look closely at the motif to check it is worked correctly and identify the features mentioned.

Motifs are usually joined to each other as the last round is worked and the pattern will explain exactly where these joining points should be, and how the motifs should be joined. Join the motifs whilst working this last round by holding the motif being worked and the one it is to be joined to with their wrong sides together and work the joining stitch as detailed in the pattern. The motifs should be joined following the diagram that shows how the motifs fit together, making sure that any extra joining points required (as detailed in the written instructions) are followed to complete the item.

WORKING AN EDGING

Crochet items often have a separate edging added afterwards to smooth out the edge and give a professional finish, and it is important that this edging is worked evenly. It can be very easy to accidentally stretch an edge whilst working along it and this will distort and spoil the work.

The first row or round of an edging is normally worked with the right side of the crochet facing. To attach the yarn to start an edging, make a slip knot and slip this over the hook. Insert the hook into the edge at the point specified in the pattern and work a slip stitch to secure the yarn. Follow the pattern to work the rest of the edging, taking great care, if working in rounds, to check whether the work needs to be turned or not at the end of each round.

Crab stitch

Almost all crochet stitches are worked from right to left but there is one common exception to this rule – crab stitch. This forms a neat corded edging and it is worked from left to right. It is basically just a row of double crochet but worked backwards.

Work a line of crab stitch by inserting the hook into the stitch to the right of the previous stitch, inserting it from front to back and making sure that the yarn is held above the hook and the work. Loop the yarn under the hook and draw this new loop of yarn through the stitch so that there are 2 loops on the hook. Take the yarn over the hook in the normal way and carefully pull this new loop through both the loops on the hook to complete the stitch. Continue along the edge, making each stitch in exactly the same way, to form a neat edging that consists of lots of knots that sit along the edge of the work.

JOINING THE CROCHETED PIECES

Once all the crocheted sections have been completed, they may need to be joined together to complete the item. To join the pieces together, use a blunt-pointed sewing needle and the same yarn as used for the crochet. Whilst it is possible to buy needles specifically designed for sewing together hand knits or crochet items, a large-eyed tapestry or cross stitch embroidery needle is just as good. Using a large blunt-pointed needle ensures that, as the seam is stitched, the fibres of the yarn used are gently eased apart, leaving room for the seaming yarn to easily slide through the work without causing any damage.

The type of stitch that should be used to join the edges together will depend on the type of crochet stitch that has been worked, the yarn that has been used and the position of the seam within the item.

Over sewing a seam

An over sewn seam will create a flat seam that, depending on the yarn and stitch pattern used, will be virtually invisible. This type of seam is particularly useful when joining fine yarns and lacy stitches.

Make the seam by holding the two edges to be joined next to each other, with their right sides facing. Carefully and neatly over sew the edges together, making stitches that are about the same size as a chain stitch would be. Once the seam has been completed, open out the two pieces and gently flatten the seam.

Back stitching a seam

Back stitch will create a seam that is strong but flexible, making it ideal for shoulder seams on large garments. However, because of the way the seam is made, it can create quite a bulky seam, so is best avoided when working with thick yarns, and it can be very difficult to work on very lacy stitch patterns.

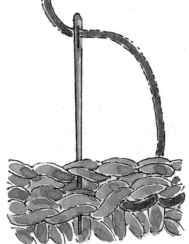

Hold the two sections to be joined with their right sides together and work a line of back stitch along the edge, making each stitch through both layers. Try to work the stitches as close as is possible to the edge of the crochet.

Crocheting a seam

Crochet sections can be joined by working a line of double crochet to create the seam. This type of seam is very strong, very flexible and, if worked correctly, will lie virtually flat, thereby not adding any bulk inside the garment.

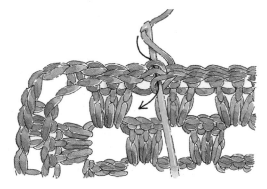

Holding the two pieces to be joined with their right sides together and using the same size hook as used for the main crochet sections, attach the yarn at one end of the seam. Now work a row of double crochet along the edges, inserting the hook through the edges of both sections when working each stitch.

FINISHING THE CROCHET

Once the crochet item is completed, it may well need to be pressed. Before pressing the work, refer to the ball band of the yarn being used to find out exactly how this should be done. This is particularly important when working with the fancy textured and the sparkly yarns featured in this book. Follow the instructions on the ball band very carefully to avoid damaging the yarn.

Regardless of the pressing instructions on the ball band, extra care must be taken if the item is decorated with beads or sequins. Even a warm iron will melt sequins and fragile glass beads could easily shatter if they come into contact with an iron.

If the beads that have been used are small and the yarn can be pressed, press the item very carefully from the wrong side of the work, protecting the beads by covering the pressing surface with layers of soft cloth that will cushion the beads – a couple of soft towels covered with an old sheet are ideal. It is also advisable to use a pressing cloth to avoid the risk of the iron damaging a stray bead that may have crept through to the wrong side of the work.

If the item has sequins attached to it, do NOT press it! If it does need to be "pressed", it can be blocked out to size. To block out the item, cover a large firm surface, such as an old table, with several towels under an old sheet or tablecloth. Pin the item out to shape on this surface, making sure all the sequins "sit" in their correct positions and making sure the item is the size detailed within the pattern. Cover the pinned-out work with another cloth and mist this cloth with water – it should be damp, not wet! Leave everything to dry naturally away from direct heat. Once totally dry, remove the cloth and the pins and the item is complete.

AFTERCARE

It is a good idea to keep an oddment of the yarn used, together with a ball band and a few spare beads or sequins, in a safe place so that this can be referred to at a later date. The ball band will give details of how the yarn should be laundered but, if beads or sequins are attached, the item should NOT be machine washed even if the yarn could be. Instead, hand wash the item very carefully in luke warm water. Alternatively, have the item dry cleaned by a professional.

BRIGHT LIGHTS

Light up a dark evening with these dynamic designs worked in a myriad of bright jewel-like colours. Passionate pinks, gorgeous greens, perfect purple, terrific turquoise, glittering gold and ruby red all combine with mouthwatering yarns to get you noticed. Some designs are encrusted with beads and others are really simple and quick to make – but all of them are guaranteed to bring a smile to everyone's face.

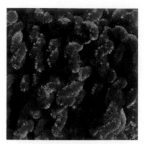

Keep cosy and warm but still look stunning in this little edge-to-edge jacket. Short and boxy, it will work up quickly in a really chunky and luscious chenille yarn – and the little loops create the cutest of ringlets!

'Fur' Jacket

★★☆ INTERMEDIATE

MEASUREMENTS

To fit bust

81	86	91	97	102	107	cm
32	34	36	38	40	42	in

Actual size

88	94	100	106	112	118	cm
$34^1/_2$	37	$39^1/_4$	$41^3/_4$	44	$46^1/_2$	in

Actual length

42	43	44	45	46	47	cm
$16^1/_2$	17	$17^1/_4$	$17^3/_4$	18	$18^1/_2$	in

Actual sleeve

43	43	44	44	44	45	cm
17	17	$17^1/_4$	$17^1/_4$	$17^1/_4$	$17^3/_4$	in

MATERIALS

- 11 (12: 13: 14: 15: 16) × 100 g balls of Sirdar Wow! in Raspberry Crush 758
- 10.00 mm crochet hook

TENSION

$6^1/_2$ sts and $6^1/_2$ rows to 10 cm (4 in) measured over pattern using 10.00 mm hook. Change hook size if necessary to obtain this tension.

ABBREVIATIONS

dc2tog – *insert hook as indicated, yoh and draw loop through, rep from * once more, yoh and draw through all 3 loops on hook;
loop 1=insert hook into next st, using finger of left hand draw out yarn to form a loop approx 10–12 cm (4–$4^1/_2$ in) long, pick up both strands of this loop with hook and draw through st, yoh and draw loop through all 3 loops on hook.

See also page 15.

BODY (worked in one piece to armholes)

With 10.00 mm hook, make 58 (62: 66: 70: 74: 78) ch.
Foundation row: (RS) 1 dc into 2nd ch from hook, 1 dc into each ch to end, turn. 57 (61: 65: 69: 73: 77) sts.
Cont in patt as follows:
Row 1: (WS) 1 ch (does NOT count as st), loop 1 into each dc to end, turn.
Row 2: 1 ch (does NOT count as st), 1 dc into each st to end, turn.
These 2 rows form patt.
Cont in patt until Body measures approx 21 (22: 22: 23: 23: 24) cm, $8^1/_4$ ($8^1/_2$: $8^1/_2$: 9: 9: $9^1/_2$) in, ending with a WS row.

Divide for armholes

Next row: (RS) 1 ch (does NOT count as st), 1 dc into each of first 12 (13: 14: 15: 16: 17) sts and turn, leaving rem sts unworked.
Work on this set of 12 (13: 14: 15: 16: 17) sts only for Right Front.

+ dc
℧ loop 1

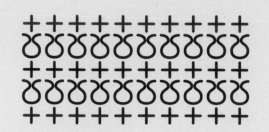

■ *Sirdar Wow! is a really chunky chenille yarn that means your crochet will grow surprisingly quickly – so your jacket will be made in less time than you may think.*

■ *The fronts and back of this jacket are worked all in one piece so you have less seams to sew up. It also means there are no bulky side seams to spoil the look of your finished garment.*

Next row: 1 ch (does NOT count as st), dc2tog over first 2 sts – 1 st decreased, loop 1 into each dc to end, turn.

Next row: 1 ch (does NOT count as st), 1 dc into each st to last 2 sts, dc2tog over last 2 sts – 1 st decreased, turn. 10 (11: 12: 13: 14: 15) sts.

Working all decreases as set by last 2 rows, dec 1 st at armhole edge on next 0 (0: 1: 1: 2: 2) rows. 10 (11: 11: 12: 12: 13) sts.

Cont straight until armhole measures approx 13 (13: 14: 14: 15: 15) cm, 5 (5: 5½: 5½: 6: 6) in, ending with a RS row.

Shape neck

Next row: (WS) 1 ch (does NOT count as st), loop 1 into each of first 7 (8: 8: 8: 8: 9) dc and turn, leaving rem 3 (3: 3: 4: 4: 4) sts unworked. Dec 1 st at neck edge on next 2 rows. 5 (6: 6: 6: 6: 7) sts.

Cont straight until armhole measures approx 21 (21: 22: 22: 23: 23) cm, 8¼ (8¼: 8½: 8½: 9: 9) in, ending with a WS row.

Shape shoulder

Fasten off.

Return to last complete row worked, miss next 4 sts, rejoin yarn to next st and cont as follows:

Next row: (RS) 1 ch (does NOT count as st), 1 dc into st where yarn was rejoined, 1 dc into each of next 24 (26: 28: 30: 32: 34) sts and turn, leaving rem sts unworked.

Work on this set of 25 (27: 29: 31: 33: 35) sts only for Back.

Dec 1 st at each end of next 2 (2: 3: 3: 4: 4) rows. 21 (23: 23: 25: 25: 27) sts.

Cont straight until Back matches Right Front to shoulder, ending with a WS row.

Shape shoulders

Fasten off, placing markers either side of centre 11 (11: 11: 13: 13: 13) sts to denote back neck.

Return to last complete row worked, miss next 4 sts, rejoin yarn to next st and cont as follows:

Next row: (RS) 1 ch (does NOT count as st), 1 dc into st where yarn was rejoined, 1 dc into each st to end, turn.

Work on this set of 12 (13: 14: 15: 16: 17) sts for Left Front.

Dec 1 st at armhole edge on next 2 (2: 3: 3: 4: 4) rows. 10 (11: 11: 12: 12: 13) sts.

Cont straight until armhole measures approx 13 (13: 14: 14: 15: 15) cm, 5 (5: 5½: 5½: 6: 6) in, ending with a RS row.

Shape neck

Next row: (WS) ss across and into 4th (4th: 4th: 5th: 5th: 5th) dc, 1 ch (does NOT count as st), loop 1 into same place as last ss, loop 1 into each dc to end, turn. 7 (8: 8: 8: 8: 9) sts.

Dec 1 st at neck edge on next 2 rows. 5 (6: 6: 6: 6: 7) sts.

Cont straight until Left Front matches Right Front to shoulder, ending with a WS row.

- Using Sirdar Wow! for a loop stitch pattern like this one will mean that all the loops will naturally fall into little ringlets. If you find one or two don't, then simply twist them so that they do!
- You might find it difficult to sew up the garment with a yarn this thick. If you do, then simply sew it up using a matching shade of a thinner yarn.
- As there are no edgings added to this garment, it's a good idea to try to keep the front opening and neck edges as neat as possible.

Shape shoulder
Fasten off.

SLEEVES
With 10.00 mm hook, make 17 (17: 18: 18: 19: 19) ch.
Work foundation row as given for Body. 16 (16: 17: 17: 18: 18) sts.
Cont in patt as given for Body as follows:
Work 3 rows, ending with a WS row.
Next row: (RS) 1 ch (does NOT count as st), 2 dc into first dc – 1 st increased, 1 dc into each st to last st, 2 dc into last st – 1 st increased, turn.
Working all increases as set by last row, inc 1 st at each end of every foll 6th row until there are 24 (24: 25: 25: 26: 26) sts.
Cont straight until Sleeve measures approx 43 (43: 44: 44: 44: 45) cm, 17 (17: 17^1/$_4$: 17^1/$_4$: 17^1/$_4$: 17^3/$_4$) in, ending with a RS row.

Shape top
Next row: (WS) ss across and into 3rd dc, 1 ch (does NOT count as st), loop 1 into same place as last ss, loop 1 into each of next 19 (19: 20: 20: 21: 21) dc and turn, leaving rem 2 dc unworked.
Dec 1 st at each end of next 7 rows, ending with a RS row. 6 (6: 7: 7: 8: 8) sts.
Fasten off.

TO MAKE UP
Do NOT press.
Join shoulder seams. Join sleeve seams. Matching top of sleeve seam to centre of sts missed at underarm and centre of last row of sleeve to shoulder seam, sew sleeves into armholes.

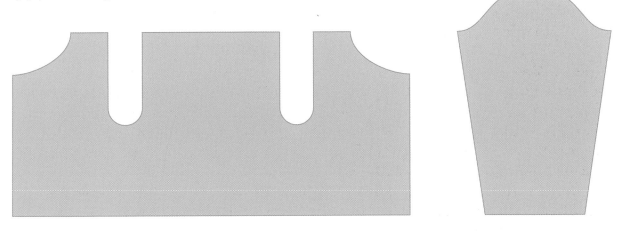

This light-as-air shrug will keep any chill breezes off your shoulders. It's worked in a pretty lacy stitch, using the most luxurious of kid mohair and silk blend yarns, and the edges are finished with a neat line of beads.

Shoulder Shrug

INTERMEDIATE ★★☆

MEASUREMENTS

To fit bust

81–86	91–97	102–107	cm
32–34	36–38	40–42	in

Actual width, at widest point

68	73	78	cm
26³/4	28³/4	30³/4	in

Actual length

41	43	45	cm
16	17	17	in

MATERIALS

- 3 (4: 4) × 25 g balls of Rowan Kidsilk Haze in Splendour 579
- 2.50 mm crochet hook
- Approx 210 (220: 230) beads

TENSION

4 patt reps and 11 rows to 10 cm (4 in) measured over pattern using 2.50 mm hook. Change hook size if necessary to obtain this tension.

ABBREVIATIONS

See page 15.

For how to work with beads, see pages 16–17.

BACK

With 2.50 mm hook, make 146 (162: 178) ch.
Foundation row: (RS) 1 dc into 2nd ch from hook, *miss 3 ch, (1 tr, 1 ch, 1 tr, 3 ch, 1 tr, 1 ch and 1 tr) into next ch, miss 3 ch, 1 dc into next ch, rep from * to end, turn. 18 (20: 22) patt reps.

Cont in patt as follows:
Row 1: (WS) 7 ch (counts as first dtr and 3 ch), miss (1 dc, 1 tr, 1 ch and 1 tr), *(1 dc, 3 ch and 1 dc) into next ch sp, 3 ch, miss (1 tr, 1 ch and 1 tr), 1 dtr into next dc**, 3 ch, miss (1 tr, 1 ch and 1 tr), rep from * to end, ending last rep at **, turn.

Row 2: 4 ch (counts as first tr and 1 ch), (1 tr, 1 ch and 1 tr) into dtr at base of 4 ch, *miss (3 ch and 1 dc), 1 dc into next ch sp, miss (1 dc and 3 ch)**, (1 tr, 1 ch, 1 tr, 3 ch, 1 tr, 1 ch and 1 tr) into next dtr, rep from * to end, ending last rep at **, (1 tr, 1 ch, 1 tr, 1 ch and 1 tr) into 4th of 7 ch at beg of previous row, turn.

Row 3: 1 ch (does NOT count as st), 1 dc into tr at end of previous row, 1 dc into next ch sp, *3 ch, miss (1 tr, 1 ch and 1 tr), 1 dtr into next dc, 3 ch, miss (1 tr, 1 ch and 1 tr)**, (1 dc, 3 ch and 1 dc) into next ch sp, rep from * to end, ending last rep at **, 1 dc into next ch sp, 1 dc into 3rd of 4 ch at beg of previous row, turn.

Designed just to cover your shoulders, this little shrug is the perfect accompaniment to a strappy dress or top. And it's made using such a lightweight yarn that you'll hardly even notice you've got it on!

Don't worry if the finished edges don't look totally straight – once the beaded edging is complete they will straighten out.

Row 4: 1 ch (does NOT count as st), 1 dc into dc at end of previous row, *miss (1 dc and 3 ch), (1 tr, 1 ch, 1 tr, 3 ch, 1 tr, 1 ch and 1 tr) into next dtr, miss (3 ch and 1 dc), 1 dc into next ch sp, rep from * to end, working last dc into dc at beg of previous row, turn. These 4 rows form patt. Work 1 row, ending with patt row 1 and a WS row.

Shape for sleeve

Next row: (RS) 4 ch (counts as first tr and 1 ch), (1 tr, 3 ch, 1 tr, 1 ch and 1 tr) into dtr at base of 4 ch - ½ patt rep increased, *miss (3 ch and 1 dc), 1 dc into next ch sp, miss (1 dc and 3 ch)**, (1 tr, 1 ch, 1 tr, 3 ch, 1 tr, 1 ch and 1 tr) into next dtr, rep from * to end, ending last rep at **, (1 tr, 1 ch, 1 tr, 3 ch, 1 tr, 1 ch and 1 tr) into 4th of 7 ch at beg of previous row – ½ patt rep increased, turn.

Next row: 7 ch (counts as first dtr and 3 ch), miss (1 tr, 1 ch and 1 tr), *(1 dc, 3 ch and 1 dc) into next ch sp, 3 ch**, miss (1 tr, 1 ch and 1 tr), 1 dtr into next dc, 3 ch, miss (1 tr, 1 ch and 1 tr), rep from * to end, ending last rep at **, miss (1 tr and 1 ch), 1 dtr into 3rd of 4 ch at beg of previous row, turn.

Rep last 2 rows 8 times more. 27 (29: 31) patt reps.

Place markers at both ends of last row to denote base of armhole opening.

Starting with patt row 2, work in patt for a further 19 (21: 23) rows, ending with patt row 4 (2: 4) and a RS row.

First and third sizes only

Next row: (WS) 7 ch (counts as first dtr and 3 ch), miss (1 dc, 1 tr, 1 ch and 1 tr), *1 dc into next ch sp, 3 ch, miss (1 tr, 1 ch and 1 tr), 1 dtr into next dc**, 3 ch, miss (1 tr, 1 ch and 1 tr), rep from * to end, ending last rep at **.

Second size only

Next row: (WS) 1 ch (does NOT count as st), 1 dc into tr at end of previous row, 1 dc into next ch sp, *3 ch, miss (1 tr, 1 ch and 1 tr), 1 dtr into next dc, 3 ch, miss (1 tr, 1 ch and 1 tr)**, 1 dc into next ch sp, rep from * to end, ending last rep at **, 1 dc into next ch sp, 1 dc into 3rd of 4 ch at beg of previous row.

All sizes

Fasten off, placing markers either side of centre 7 (8: 9) patt reps to denote back neck.

LEFT FRONT

With 2.50 mm hook, make 10 ch.
Work foundation row as given for Back.
1 patt rep.
Starting with patt row 1, cont in patt as given for Back as follows:
Work 1 row, ending with patt row 1 and a WS row.

Shape front opening edge

Working all shaping as given for Back, inc ½ patt rep at end of next and foll alt row. 2 patt reps.
Work 1 row. (6 rows completed.)

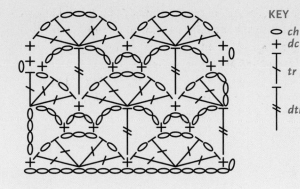

KEY

ch
dc
tr
dtr

- The beads around the edges are quite large – but you could easily use smaller ones. Whatever size you use, try to make sure they are not too heavy as to weigh the garment down and pull it out of shape.
- This yarn is a luxurious blend of kid mohair and silk that creates a superb fine yarn that is surprisingly easy to crochet with.
- Once your garment is complete, there's no need to press it. Just shake it out quite vigorously to raise the pile of the mohair and wear it!

Shape for sleeve

Inc $1/2$ patt rep at beg of next and foll alt row. 3 patt reps.

Work 1 row.

Inc $1/2$ patt rep at each end of next and foll alt row. 5 patt reps.

Work 1 row.

Rep last 8 rows once more. 8 patt reps.

Inc $1/2$ patt rep at beg of next row. $8^1/2$ patt reps.

Work 1 row.

Place marker at end of last row to denote base of armhole opening.

Work 2 rows.

Now keeping armhole opening edge straight, inc $1/2$ patt rep at front opening edge of next and foll alt row. $9^1/2$ patt reps.

Work 5 rows.

Second and third sizes only

Rep last 8 rows once more. $10^1/2$ patt reps.

First and third sizes only

Inc $1/2$ patt rep at end of next row. 10 (11) patt reps.

All sizes

Work 9 (4: 5) rows, replacing the (1 dc, 3 ch and 1 dc) into ch sp with (1 dc) as given for last row of Back. Fasten off.

RIGHT FRONT

Work as given for Left Front, reversing all shaping.

TO MAKE UP

Do NOT press.

Join shoulder/overarm seams. Join side seams below markers.

Edging

Thread beads onto yarn.

With 2.50 mm hook, rejoin yarn at base of one side seam, 1 ch (does NOT count as st), work 1 round of dc evenly around entire hem, front opening and neck edges, ending with ss to first dc and ensuring number of sts worked is divisible by 4, **turn.**

Next round: (WS) 1 ch (does NOT count as st), 1 dc into first dc, *1 beaded dc into next dc, 1 dc into each of next 3 dc, rep from * to last 3 dc, 1 beaded dc into next dc, 1 dc into each of last 2 dc, ss to first dc.

Fasten off.

Work Edging around armhole opening edges in same way, rejoining yarn at top of side seam.

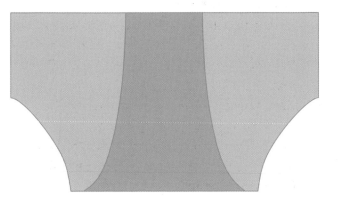

This poncho is really simple to make – it's just sixteen big and lacy motifs! Worked in a stunning hand-dyed ribbon yarn, it'll definitely make you the belle of the ball.

Poncho

MEASUREMENTS

One size, to fit bust
86–107 cm
34–42 in

Actual size, at widest point
85 cm
33¹/₂ in

Actual length, from nape of neck
71 cm
28 in

MATERIALS

- 3 × 100g hanks of Colinette Giotto in Rio 140
- 7.00 mm crochet hook

TENSION

Motif measures 20 cm (7³/₄ in) square on 7.00 mm hook. Change hook size if necessary to obtain this tension.

ABBREVIATIONS

tr2tog – *yoh and insert hook as indicated, yoh and draw loop through, yoh and draw through 2 loops, rep from * once more, yoh and draw through all 3 loops on hook; **tr3tog** – *yoh and insert hook as indicated, yoh and draw loop through, yoh and draw through 2 loops, rep from * twice more, yoh and draw through all 4 loops on hook. *See also page 15.*

MOTIF

With 7.00 mm hook, make 6 ch and join with a ss to form a ring.

Round 1: (RS) 1 ch (does NOT count as st), [1 dc into ring, 15 ch] 12 times, ss to first dc. 12 ch sps.

Round 2: ss into each of first 7 ch of first ch sp, 3 ch (does NOT count as st), (tr2tog, 4 ch and tr3tog) into same ch sp, *[4 ch, 1 dc into next ch sp] twice, 4 ch**, (tr3tog, 4 ch and tr3tog) into next ch sp, rep from * to end, ending last rep at **, ss to top of tr2tog at beg of round.

Round 3: ss into first ch sp, 3 ch (does NOT count as st), (tr2tog, 5 ch and tr3tog) into same ch sp, *5 ch, 1 dc into next ch sp, 5 ch, tr3tog into next ch sp, 5 ch, 1 dc into next ch sp, 5 ch**, (tr3tog, 5 ch and tr3tog) into next ch sp, rep from * to end, ending last rep at **, ss to top of tr2tog at beg of round.
Fasten off.

Basic Motif is a square. In each corner there is a 5-ch sp between a pair of tr3tog, and along sides there are a further four 5-ch sps. Join Motifs whilst working Round 3 at corners, by replacing corner (5 ch) with (2 ch, 1 ss into corner 5-ch sp of adjacent Motif, 2 ch), and at side ch sps, by replacing (5 ch) with (2 ch, 1 ss into corresponding ch sp of adjacent Motif, 2 ch).

Following diagram, make and join 16 Basic Motifs to form shape shown. Join second overarm/side seam whilst joining Motifs as indicated by arrows.

Neck Edging

With 7.00 mm hook and RS facing, attach yarn at point A on diagram and work around neck edge as follows: 1 ch (does NOT count as st), 1 dc into joining point of Motifs – this is where yarn was rejoined, *2 ch, 1 dc into next ch sp, [3 ch, 1 dc into next ch sp] 3 times, 2 ch, 1 dc into next joining point, rep from * to end, replacing dc at end of last rep with ss to first dc, turn.

Next round: (WS) 1 ch (does NOT count as st), 2 dc into first ch sp, *[1 dc into next dc, 3 dc into next ch sp] 3 times, 1 dc into next dc, 2 dc into next ch sp, miss next dc, rep from * to end, ss to first dc.
Fasten off.

TO MAKE UP

Do NOT press.

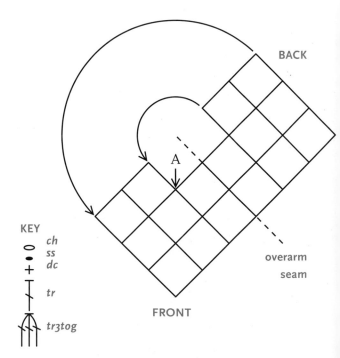

KEY
∘ ch
• ss
+ dc
⊤ tr
⋔ tr3tog

Knock 'em dead in this sexy little top! Made in a delicate openwork lacy stitch using a shimmering kid mohair yarn with a touch of lurex, the edges are trimmed with glittering beads to complete the look.

Tie Front Cardigan

INTERMEDIATE ★★☆

MEASUREMENTS

To fit bust

76–81	81–86	91–97	97–102	107–112	cm
30–32	32–34	36–38	38–40	42–44	in

Actual size

85	93	101	108	116	cm
33^1/$_2$	36^1/$_2$	39^3/$_4$	42^1/$_2$	45^1/$_2$	in

Actual length

52	52	53	55	55	cm
20^1/$_2$	20^1/$_2$	20^3/$_4$	21^1/$_2$	21^1/$_2$	in

Actual sleeve

46	46	46	46	46	cm
18	18	18	18	18	in

MATERIALS

- 6 (7: 8: 9: 10) × 25 g balls of Rowan Kidsilk Night in Dazzle 609
- 3.50 mm crochet hook
- Approx 510 (520: 560: 600: 620) beads

TENSION

26 sts and 13 rows to 10 cm (4 in) measured over pattern using 3.50 mm hook. Change hook size if necessary to obtain this tension.

ABBREVIATIONS

See page 15.

For how to work with beads, see pages 16–17.

BACK

With 3.50 mm hook, make 112 (122: 132: 142: 152) ch.

Foundation row: (RS) 1 dc into 2nd ch from hook, 1 dc into next ch, *miss 3 ch, (3 tr, 1 ch and 3 tr) into next ch, miss 3 ch, 1 dc into next ch**, 1 ch, miss 1 ch, 1 dc into next ch, rep from * to end, ending last rep at **, 1 dc into last ch, turn. 111 (121: 131: 141: 151) sts, 11 (12: 13: 14: 15) patt reps.

Cont in patt as follows:

Row 1: (WS) 2 ch (counts as first htr), 1htr into dc at base of 2 ch, *3 ch, miss (1 dc and 3 tr), 1 dc into next ch sp, 3 ch, miss (3 tr and 1 dc)**, (1 htr, 1 ch and 1 htr) into next ch sp, rep from * to end, ending last rep at **, 2 htr into last dc, turn.

Row 2: 3 ch (counts as first tr), 3 tr into htr at base of 3 ch, *miss 1 htr, 1 dc into next ch sp, 1 ch, miss 1 dc, 1 dc into next ch sp, miss 1 htr**, (3 tr, 1 ch and 3 tr) into next ch sp, rep from * to end, ending last rep at **, 4 tr into top of 2 ch at beg of previous row, turn.

Row 3: 1 ch (does NOT count as st), 1 dc into last tr of previous row, *3 ch, miss (3 tr and 1 dc), (1 htr, 1 ch and 1 htr) into next ch sp, 3 ch, miss (1 dc and 3 tr), 1 dc into next ch sp, rep from * to end, working dc at end of last rep into top of 3 ch at beg of previous row, turn.

Row 4: 1 ch (does NOT count as st), 1 dc into dc at end of previous row, *1 dc into next ch sp, miss 1 htr, (3 tr, 1 ch and 3 tr) into next ch sp, miss 1 htr, 1 dc into next ch sp**, 1 ch, miss 1 dc, rep from * to end, ending last rep at **, 1 dc into last dc, turn.

These 4 rows form patt.

Cont in patt for a further 36 rows, ending with patt row 4 and a RS row. (Back should measure 32 cm, 12^1/$_2$ in.)

Shape armholes

Next row: (WS) ss across first 2 dc, next 3 tr and into next ch sp, 1 ch (does NOT count as st), 1 dc into same ch sp as last ss - ^{1}/$_2$ patt rep decreased, *3 ch, miss (3 tr and 1 dc), (1 htr, 1 ch and 1 htr) into next ch sp, 3 ch, miss (1 dc and 3 tr), 1 dc into next ch sp, rep from * until dc has been worked into ch sp between last group of trs and turn, leaving rem (3 tr and 2 dc) unworked – ^{1}/$_2$ patt rep decreased.

Next row: As patt row 4.

Rep last 2 rows 2 (2: 3: 3: 4) times more. 8 (9: 9: 10: 10) patt reps.

Work a further 19 (19: 19: 21: 19) rows, ending with a WS row. (Armhole should measure 19 (19: 20: 22: 22) cm, 7^1/$_2$ (7^1/$_2$: 8: 8^1/$_2$: 8^1/$_2$) in.)

Fasten off, placing markers 2 (2^1/$_2$: 2^1/$_2$: 2^1/$_2$: 2^1/$_2$) patt reps in from each end of last row to denote back neck – there should be 4 (4: 4: 5: 5) patt reps across back neck.

LEFT FRONT

With 3.50 mm hook, make 162 (172: 182: 192: 202) ch.

Work foundation row as given for Back. 161 (171: 181: 191: 201) sts, 16 (17: 18: 19: 20) patt reps.

Cont in patt as given for Back follows:

Work 4 rows, ending with patt row 4 and a RS row.

Shape tie

Working all shaping as given for Back, dec ^{1}/$_2$ patt rep at beg of next row. 15^1/$_2$ (16^1/$_2$: 17^1/$_2$: 18^1/$_2$: 19^1/$_2$) patt reps.

Dec 4 patt reps at end of next row (by simply leaving last 4 patt reps unworked – row should end in same way as patt row 4 ends). 11^1/$_2$ (12^1/$_2$: 13^1/$_2$: 14^1/$_2$: 15^1/$_2$) patt reps.

Dec ^{1}/$_2$ patt rep at beg of next and foll 9 (11: 12: 14: 16) alt rows, then on 2 (1: 1: 0: 0) foll 6th rows. 5^1/$_2$ (6: 6^1/$_2$: 7: 7) patt reps.

***Work 3 (5: 3: 5: 1) row. (Left Front should now match back to start of armhole shaping.)

Shape armhole

Dec ^{1}/$_2$ patt rep at armhole edge of next and foll 2 (2: 3: 3: 4) alt rows and at same time dec ^{1}/$_2$ patt rep at front slope edge on 3rd (next: 3rd: next: 5th) and foll 0 (0: 0: 6th: 0) row. 3^1/$_2$ (4: 4: 4: 4) patt reps.

Dec ^{1}/$_2$ patt rep at front slope edge only on 4th (2nd: 2nd: 6th: 2nd) and every foll 6th row until 2 (2^1/$_2$: 2^1/$_2$: 2^1/$_2$: 2^1/$_2$) patt reps rem.

Work a further 4 (6: 6: 4: 6) rows, ending with a WS row. (Left Front should match Back to fasten-off row.)
Fasten off.

RIGHT FRONT

Work as given for Left Front to start of tie shaping.

Shape tie

Working all shaping as given for Back, dec $1/2$ patt rep at end of next row. $15^1/2$ ($16^1/2$: $17^1/2$: $18^1/2$: $19^1/2$) patt reps.

Dec 4 patt reps at beg of next row (by simply breaking yarn and re-joining it 4 patt reps further along row – row should begin in same way as patt row 4 begins). $11^1/2$ ($12^1/2$: $13^1/2$: $14^1/2$: $15^1/2$) patt reps.

Dec $1/2$ patt rep at end of next and foll 9 (11: 12: 14: 16) alt rows, then on 2 (1: 1: 0: 0) foll 6th rows. $5^1/2$ (6: $6^1/2$: 7: 7) patt reps.

Complete as given for Left Front from ***.

SLEEVES

With 3.50 mm hook, make 52 (52: 62: 72: 72) ch. Work foundation row as given for Back. 51 (51: 61: 71: 71) sts, 5 (5: 6: 7: 7) patt reps.

Cont in patt as given for Back follows:

Work 9 rows, ending with patt row 1 and a WS row.

Next row: (RS) 3 ch (counts as first tr), (3 tr, 1 ch and 3 tr) into htr at base of 3 ch, *miss 1 htr, 1 dc into next ch sp, 1 ch, miss 1 dc, 1 dc into next ch sp, miss 1 htr**, (3 tr, 1 ch and 3 tr) into next ch sp, rep from * to end, ending last rep at **, (3 tr, 1 ch and 4 tr) into top of 2 ch at beg of previous row, turn.

Next row: 2 ch (counts as first htr), 1htr into tr at base of 2 ch – $1/2$ patt rep increased, 3 ch, miss 3 tr, *1 dc into next ch sp, 3 ch**, miss (3 tr and 1 dc), (1 htr, 1 ch and 1 htr) into next ch sp, 3 ch, miss (1 dc and 3 tr), rep from * to end, ending last rep at **, miss 3 tr, 2 htr into top of 3 ch at beg of previous row – $1/2$ patt rep increased, turn. 6 (6: 7: 8: 8) patt reps.

Starting with patt row 2, work 12 rows, ending with patt row 1 and a RS row.

Rep last 14 rows twice more. 8 (8: 9: 10: 10) patt reps.

Work a further 7 rows, ending with patt row 4 and a WS row. (Sleeve should measure 45 cm, $17^3/4$ in.)

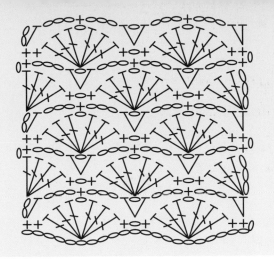

KEY

o	ch
+	dc
T	htr
$\mathbf{\overline{T}}$	tr

Shape top

Working all shaping as given for Back, dec ½ patt rep at each end of next and foll 5 (5: 6: 7: 7) alt rows. 2 patt reps.
Fasten off.

TO MAKE UP

Do NOT press.
Join shoulder and side seams. Join sleeve seams. Sew Sleeves into armholes.

Edging

Thread beads onto yarn.
With 3.50 mm hook, rejoin yarn at base of one side seam, 1 ch (does NOT count as st), work 1 round of dc evenly around entire hem, tie, front opening and neck edges, ending with ss to first dc and ensuring an even number of sts are worked, **turn**.
Next round: (WS) 1 ch (does NOT count as st), *1 dc into next dc, 1 beaded dc into next dc, rep from * to end, ss to first dc, turn.
Next round: 1 ch (does NOT count as st), 1 dc into each st to end, ss to first dc.
Fasten off.
Work Edging around lower edge of Sleeves in same way, rejoining yarn at base of sleeve seam.

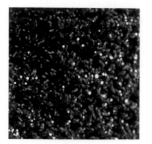

This little funnel neck top, with its cut-away armholes, is gently fitted to flatter your figure. Made using a fine lurex yarn, it uses a clever textured stitch that is easy to work. And it will look just as good with jeans as with the poshest of skirts.

Sleeveless Top

★★☆ INTERMEDIATE

MEASUREMENTS

To fit bust

81	86	91	97	102	107	cm
32	34	36	38	40	42	
in						

Actual size, at underarm

85	88	95	99	106	110	cm
33^1/$_2$	34^1/$_2$	37^1/$_2$	39	41^3/$_4$	43^1/$_4$	in

Actual length

52	53	55	57	59	60	cm
20^1/$_2$	20^3/$_4$	22^1/$_2$	22^1/$_2$	23^1/$_4$	23^1/$_2$	in

MATERIALS

- 7 (7: 8: 9: 9: 10) × 50 g balls of Twilleys Goldfingering in purple 60
- 2.50 mm crochet hook

TENSION

34 sts and 17 rows to 10 cm (4 in) measured over pattern using 2.50 mm hook. Change hook size if necessary to obtain this tension.

ABBREVIATIONS

See page 15.

BACK

With 2.50 mm hook, make 146 (152: 164: 170: 182: 188) ch.

Foundation row: (RS) 1 dc into 2nd ch from hook, *miss 2 ch, (1 tr, 1 ch, 1 tr, 1 ch and 1 tr) into next ch, miss 2 ch, 1 dc into next ch, rep from * to end, turn. 145 (151: 163: 169: 181: 187) sts, 24 (25: 27: 28: 30: 31) patt reps.

Cont in patt as follows:

Row 1: (WS) 4 ch (counts as 1 tr and 1 ch), 1 tr into dc at base of 4 ch, *miss (1 tr and 1 ch), 1 dc into next tr, miss (1 ch and 1 tr)**, (1 tr, 1 ch, 1 tr, 1 ch and 1 tr) into next dc, rep from * to end, ending last rep at **, (1 tr, 1 ch and 1 tr) into last dc, turn.

Row 2: 1 ch (does NOT count as st), 1 dc into tr at end of previous row, *miss (1 ch and 1 tr), (1 tr, 1 ch, 1 tr, 1 ch and 1 tr) into next dc, miss (1 tr and 1 ch), 1 dc into next tr, rep from * to end, working dc at end of last rep into 3rd of 4 ch at beg of previous row, turn.

These 2 rows form patt.

Keeping patt correct, cont as follows:

Work 2 rows, ending with a RS row.

Next row: (WS) ss across (first dc, 1 tr, 1 ch) and into next tr, 1 ch (does NOT count as st), 1 dc into tr at base of 1 ch – ^{1}/$_2$ patt rep decreased, patt until dc has been worked into tr at centre of last patt rep and turn, leaving

■ *Twilleys Goldfingering is a fine lurex yarn that comes in a really wide range of colours. Choose a bright strong colour, like this purple, or fuchsia or turquoise, or a soft subdued metallic shade of gold or silver. And look out for the multi coloured shades too!*

■ *The armhole edges might seem a little uneven before the edging has been worked. But don't worry – once the edgings have been added they should appear smooth and even.*

■ *It can be quite difficult to count the actual stitches when working a stitch pattern like this one – so count the number of pattern repeats instead.*

(1 ch, 1 tr and 1 dc) unworked – ½ patt rep decreased. 23 (24: 26: 27: 29: 30) patt reps. Working all decreases as set by last row, dec ½ patt rep at each end of 5th and foll 5th row. 21 (22: 24: 25: 27: 28) patt reps. Work 12 rows, ending with patt row 2.

Next row: 3 ch (counts as first st), (1 tr, 1 ch, 1 tr, 1 ch and 1 tr) into dc at base of 3 ch – ½ patt rep increased, patt to end, working (1 tr, 1 ch, 1 tr, 1 ch and **2** tr) into last dc – ½ patt rep increased, turn. 22 (23: 25: 26: 28: 29) patt reps.

Next row: 4 ch (counts as 1 tr and 1 ch), 1 tr into tr at base of 4 ch, *miss (1 tr and 1 ch), 1 dc into next tr, miss (1 ch and 1 tr)**, (1 tr, 1 ch, 1 tr, 1 ch and 1 tr) into next dc, rep from * to end, ending last rep at **, (1 tr, 1 ch and 1 tr) into top of 3 ch at beg of previous row, turn. Working all increases as now set, cont as follows: Work 5 rows.

Inc ½ patt rep at each end of next and foll 7th row. 24 (25: 27: 28: 30: 31) patt reps.

Cont straight until Back measures 33 cm, 13 in, ending with patt row 2.

Shape armholes

Dec ½ patt rep at each end of next and every foll 3rd row until 85 (85: 91: 91: 97: 97) sts, 14 (14: 15: 15: 16: 16) patt reps rem. Work 2 rows.

Fasten off, placing markers either side of centre 59 (59: 65: 65: 71: 71) sts to denote back neck.

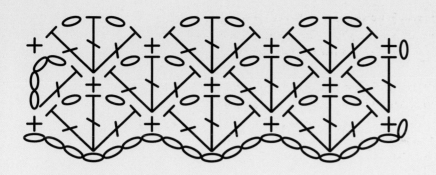

KEY

o   ch
+   dc
T   tr

FRONT

Work as given for Back until 103 (103: 109: 109: 115: 115) sts, 17 (17: 18: 18: 19: 19) patt reps rem in armhole shaping.

Shape neck

Next row: Patt 31 sts and turn, leaving rem sts unworked.

Work 1 row.

Dec ½ patt rep at each end of next and every foll 3rd row until 13 sts, 2 patt reps rem.

Work 2 rows.

Fasten off.

Return to last complete row worked, miss centre 41 (41: 47: 47: 53: 53) sts, rejoin yarn to next st, 4 ch (counts as 1 tr and 1 ch), 1 tr into dc at base of 4 ch, patt to end. 31 sts. Complete to match first side.

TO MAKE UP

Do NOT press.

Join left shoulder seam.

Neck Border

With RS facing and 2.50 mm hook, rejoin yarn at right neck shoulder point of Back, 4 ch (counts as 1 tr and 1 ch), 1 tr into dc at base of 4 ch, work until 10 (10: 11: 11: 12: 12) patt reps have been completed across back neck as set, 3 patt reps down left side of front neck, 7 (7: 8: 8: 9: 9) patt reps across front as set, then 3 patt reps up right side of neck, turn. 23 (23: 25: 25: 27: 27) patt reps.

Cont in patt as now set for a further 8 rows.

Fasten off.

Join right shoulder and Neck Border seam.

Join side seams.

Armhole Borders (Both alike)

With RS facing and 2.50 mm hook, rejoin yarn at top of one side seam, 1 ch (does NOT count as st), work 1 round of dc evenly around entire armhole edge, ending with ss to first dc, turn.

Next round: (WS) 1 ch (does NOT count as st), 1 dc into each dc to end, ss to first dc.

Fasten off.

Hem Border

With RS facing and 2.50 mm hook, rejoin yarn at base of one side seam, 1 ch (does NOT count as st), work 1 round of dc evenly around entire lower edge, ending with ss to first dc, turn.

Next round: (WS) 1 ch (does NOT count as st), 1 dc into each dc to end, ss to first dc.

Fasten off.

Combine textures and colours to create the simplest of shawls to keep you covered up and cosy. Don't let the fancy yarn put you off – it's really easy to make and you'll have it finished in no time at all!

Mini Shawl

MEASUREMENTS

Actual size
40 × 136 cm
15³/₄ × 53¹/₂ in

MATERIALS

- 5 × 50 g balls of Sirdar Frenzy in Chartreuse 777
- 10.00 mm crochet hook

TENSION

8 sts and 4¹/₂ rows to 10 cm (4 in) measured over pattern using 10.00 mm hook. Change hook size if necessary to obtain this tension.

ABBREVIATIONS

See page 15.

With 10.00 mm hook, make 4 ch.
Row 1: (RS) 1 tr into 4th ch from hook, turn. 2 sts.
Row 2: 3 ch (counts as first tr), miss tr at base of 3 ch, 2 tr between tr just missed and 3 ch at beg of previous row, turn. 3 sts.
Row 3: 3 ch (counts as first tr), miss tr at base of 3 ch, 2 tr between tr just missed and next tr, miss 1 tr, 1 tr between tr just missed and 3 ch at beg of previous row, turn. 4 sts.
Row 4: 3 ch (counts as first tr), miss tr at base of 3 ch and next tr, 2 tr between tr just missed and next tr, miss 1 tr, 2 tr between tr just missed and 3 ch at beg of previous row, turn. 5 sts.

Row 5: 3 ch (counts as first tr), miss tr at base of 3 ch, 2 tr between tr just missed and next tr, miss 2 tr, 2 tr between tr just missed and next tr, miss 1 tr, 1 tr between tr just missed and 3 ch at beg of previous row, turn. 6 sts.
Row 6: 3 ch (counts as first tr), miss tr at base of 3 ch and next tr, 2 tr between tr just missed and next tr, miss 2 tr, 2 tr between tr just missed and next tr, miss 1 tr, 2 tr between tr just missed and 3 ch at beg of previous row, turn. 7 sts.
Row 7: 3 ch (counts as first tr), miss tr at base of 3 ch, 2 tr between tr just missed and next tr, [miss 2 tr, 2 tr between tr just missed and next tr] twice, miss 1 tr, 1 tr between tr just missed and 3 ch at beg of previous row, turn. 8 sts.
Row 8: 3 ch (counts as first tr), miss tr at base of 3 ch and next tr, 2 tr between tr just missed and next tr, [miss 2 tr, 2 tr between tr just missed and next tr] twice, miss 1 tr, 2 tr between tr just missed and 3 ch at beg of previous row, turn. 9 sts.
Row 9: 3 ch (counts as first tr), miss tr at base of 3 ch, 2 tr between tr just missed and next tr, [miss 2 tr, 2 tr between tr just missed and next

■ The little ribbon "tufts" of this yarn can have a tendency to get caught in with the stitches as you work. Don't worry about this while you're crocheting – afterwards simply ease them out of the stitches using a blunt sewing-up or a fine knitting needle.

■ This shawl is surprisingly easy to make – even in a shaggy yarn like this one – as the stitches are mostly placed between the stitches of the previous rows, making it much easier to work out where to insert the crochet hook.

tr] 3 times, miss 1 tr, 1 tr between tr just missed and 3 ch at beg of previous row, turn. 10 sts.

Row 10: 3 ch (counts as first tr), miss tr at base of 3 ch and next tr, 2 tr between tr just missed and next tr, [miss 2 tr, 2 tr between tr just missed and next tr] 3 times, miss 1 tr, 2 tr between tr just missed and 3 ch at beg of previous row, turn. 11 sts.

Row 11: 3 ch (counts as first tr), miss tr at base of 3 ch, 2 tr between tr just missed and next tr, [miss 2 tr, 2 tr between tr just missed and next tr] 4 times, miss 1 tr, 1 tr between tr just missed and 3 ch at beg of previous row, turn. 12 sts.

Row 12: 3 ch (counts as first tr), miss tr at base of 3 ch and next tr, 2 tr between tr just missed and next tr, [miss 2 tr, 2 tr between tr just missed and next tr] 4 times, miss 1 tr, 2 tr between tr just missed and 3 ch at beg of previous row, turn. 13 sts.

Row 13: 3 ch (counts as first tr), miss tr at base of 3 ch, 2 tr between tr just missed and next tr, [miss 2 tr, 2 tr between tr just missed and next tr] 5 times, miss 1 tr, 1 tr between tr just missed and 3 ch at beg of previous row, turn. 14 sts.

Row 14: 3 ch (counts as first tr), miss tr at base of 3 ch and next tr, 2 tr between tr just missed and next tr, [miss 2 tr, 2 tr between tr just missed and next tr] 5 times, miss 1 tr, 2 tr between tr just missed and 3 ch at beg of previous row, turn. 15 sts.

Cont in this way, working 1 more tr on every row as now set, until the following row has been worked:

KEY

○ ch

† tr

■ *Pressing a yarn like this one would spoil the texture of it. So, once your shawl is complete, simply shake it out to raise the pile, and wear it!*

■ *This little shawl will look just as good worn round your shoulders, forming a cosy "collar", as it will if you tie it loosely round your hips and wear it is as a big sash-style belt.*

Row 31: 3 ch (counts as first tr), miss tr at base of 3 ch, 2 tr between tr just missed and next tr, [miss 2 tr, 2 tr between tr just missed and next tr] 14 times, miss 1 tr, 1 tr between tr just missed and 3 ch at beg of previous row, turn. 32 sts.

Row 32: 3 ch (counts as first tr), miss tr at base of 3 ch and next tr, 2 tr between tr just missed and next tr, [miss 2 tr, 2 tr between tr just missed and next tr] 14 times, turn, leaving last 2 tr unworked. 31 sts.

Row 33: 3 ch (counts as first tr), miss tr at base of 3 ch and next 2 tr, 2 tr between tr just missed and next tr, [miss 2 tr, 2 tr between tr just missed and next tr] 13 times, miss 1 tr, 1 tr between tr just missed and 3 ch at beg of previous row, turn. 30 sts.

Row 34: 3 ch (counts as first tr), miss tr at base of 3 ch and next tr, 2 tr between tr just missed and next tr, [miss 2 tr, 2 tr between tr just missed and next tr] 13 times, turn, leaving last 2 tr unworked. 29 sts.

Row 35: 3 ch (counts as first tr), miss tr at base of 3 ch and next 2 tr, 2 tr between tr just missed and next tr, [miss 2 tr, 2 tr between tr just missed and next tr] 12 times, miss 1 tr, 1 tr between tr just missed and 3 ch at beg of previous row, turn. 28 sts.

Row 36: 3 ch (counts as first tr), miss tr at base of 3 ch and next tr, 2 tr between tr just missed and next tr, [miss 2 tr, 2 tr between tr just missed and next tr] 12 times, turn, leaving last 2 tr unworked. 27 sts.

Row 37: 3 ch (counts as first tr), miss tr at base of 3 ch and next 2 tr, 2 tr between tr just missed and next tr, [miss 2 tr, 2 tr between tr just missed and next tr] 11 times, miss 1 tr, 1 tr between tr just missed and 3 ch at beg of previous row, turn. 26 sts.

Row 38: 3 ch (counts as first tr), miss tr at base of 3 ch and next tr, 2 tr between tr just missed and next tr, [miss 2 tr, 2 tr between tr just missed and next tr] 11 times, turn, leaving last 2 tr unworked. 25 sts.

Cont in this way, working 1 less tr on every row as now set, until the following row has been worked:

Row 58: 3 ch (counts as first tr), miss tr at base of 3 ch and next tr, 2 tr between tr just missed and next tr, miss 2 tr, 2 tr between tr just missed and next tr, turn, leaving last 2 tr unworked. 5 sts.

Row 59: 3 ch (counts as first tr), miss tr at base of 3 ch and next 2 tr, 2 tr between tr just missed and next tr, miss 1 tr, 1 tr between tr just missed and 3 ch at beg of previous row, turn. 4 sts.

Row 60: 3 ch (counts as first tr), miss tr at base of 3 ch and next tr, 2 tr between tr just missed and next tr, turn, leaving last 2 tr unworked. 3 sts.

Row 61: 3 ch (counts as first tr), miss tr at base of 3 ch and next tr, 1 tr between tr just missed and 3 ch at beg of previous row. 2 sts.
Fasten off.

TO MAKE UP
Do NOT press.

Tubes of bead-encrusted simple double crochet are all you need to make this stunning jewellery. Make your necklace as long or as short as you like, and choose beads to match your outfit. Or why not make a whole wardrobe of bracelets and necklaces?

Bracelet and Necklace

★★☆ INTERMEDIATE

MEASUREMENTS

BRACELET

Circumference
20 cm
7³/₄ in

NECKLACE

Length when fastened
42 cm
16¹/₂ in

MATERIALS

Bracelet and Necklace
- 1 × 50 g ball of Twilleys Goldfingering in red 38
- 2.50 mm crochet hook
- Approx 1,200 beads
- 1 button for Necklace

TENSION

26 sts and 30 rows to 10 cm (4 in) measured over beaded double crochet fabric using 2.50 mm hook. Change hook size if necessary to obtain this tension.

ABBREVIATIONS

See page 15.

For how to work with beads, see pages 16–17.

BRACELET

With 2.50 mm hook, make 6 ch and join with a ss to form a ring
Foundation round: (WS) 1 ch (does NOT count as st), 1 dc into each ch to end.
Cont in patt as follows:
Round 1: (WS) 1 beaded dc into each dc to end.
Round 2: (WS) 1 beaded dc into each beaded dc to end. Round 2 forms patt.**
Cont in spiralling rounds of beaded dc until strip is approx 20 cm (7³/₄ in) long – check this length is long enough that, when the ends are joined, bracelet will fit over hand.
Fasten off.

TO MAKE UP

Do NOT press.
Join ends of strip.

NECKLACE

Work as given for Bracelet to **.
Cont in spiralling rounds of beaded dc until strip is 42 cm (16¹/₂ in) long.
Now work buttonloop as follows: 7 beaded ch, ss to opposite side of last round.
Fasten off.

KEY
- ○ *ch*
- ● *ss*
- + *dc*
- ⊕ *beaded dc*

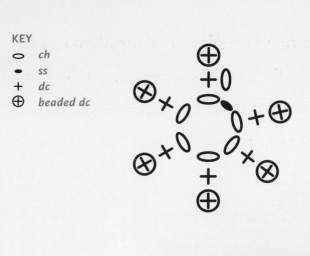

TO MAKE UP
Do NOT press.
Sew ends of strip closed, making sure buttonloop is left free. Attach button to other end of strip.

Combine glittering lurex yarn and sparkling beads to create this pull-on hat and matching skinny scarf. Made in a simple lacy stitch, the edges are finished with a scallop edging – and all sprinkled with beads!

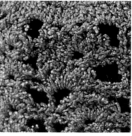

Skinny Scarf and Hat

MEASUREMENTS

SCARF

Actual size
13 × 243 cm
5 × 95¹/₂ in

HAT

Width around head
44 cm
17¹/₄ in

MATERIALS

- 4 × 50 g balls of Twilleys Goldfingering in emerald green 34
- 2.50 mm crochet hook
- Approx 2,500 beads

TENSION

3 pattern repeats (30 sts) measure 9.5 cm (3³/₄ in) and 12 rows to 10 cm (4 in) measured over pattern using 2.50 mm hook. Change hook size if necessary to obtain this tension.

ABBREVIATIONS

dc2tog – *insert hook as indicated, yoh and draw loop through, rep from * once more, yoh and draw through all 3 loops on hook; **tr2tog** – *yoh and insert hook as indicated, yoh and draw loop through, yoh and draw through 2 loops, rep from * once more, yoh and draw through all 3 loops on hook.
See also page 15.

For how to work with beads, see pages 16–17.

SCARF

Thread beads onto yarn.
With 2.50 mm hook, make 32 ch.
Foundation row: (WS) 1 dc into 2nd ch from hook, *3 ch, miss 3 ch, 1 dc into next ch, 3 ch, miss 1 ch, 1 dc into next ch, 3 ch, miss 3 ch, 1 dc into next ch, rep from * to end, turn.
3 patt reps.
Next row: 1 ch (does NOT count as st), 1 dc into first dc, *1 ch, miss (3 ch and 1 dc), tr2tog into next ch sp, [1 ch, 1 beaded ch, 1 ch and tr2tog] 4 times into same ch sp, 1 ch, miss (1 dc and 3 ch), 1 dc into next dc, rep from * to end, turn.
Cont in patt as follows:
Row 1: (WS) 7 ch (counts as first dtr and 3 ch), miss (dc at base of 7 ch, 1 ch, tr2tog, 1 ch, 1 beaded ch, 1 ch and tr2tog), *1 dc into next ch sp working dc after beaded ch, 3 ch, miss tr2tog, 1 dc into next ch sp working dc before

⊖	ch
◎	beaded ch
+	dc
⟨↑⟩	tr2tog
╪	dtr

beaded ch, 3 ch, miss (tr2tog, 1 ch, 1 beaded ch, 1 ch, tr2tog and 1 ch), 1 dtr into next dc**, 3 ch, (miss (1 ch, tr2tog, 1 ch, 1 beaded ch, 1 ch and tr2tog), rep from * to end, ending last rep at **, turn.

Row 2: 1 ch (does NOT count as st), 1 dc into first dtr, *1 ch, miss (3 ch and 1 dc), tr2tog into next ch sp, [1 ch, 1 beaded ch, 1 ch and tr2tog] 4 times into same ch sp, 1 ch, miss (1 dc and 3 ch), 1 dc into next dtr, rep from * to end, working dc at end of last rep into 4th of 7 ch at beg of previous row, turn.

These 2 rows form patt.

Cont in patt until Scarf measures approx 240 cm (94¹⁄₂ in), ending with patt row 2 and a RS row.

Next row: (WS) 7 ch (counts as first dtr and 3 ch), miss (dc at base of 7 ch, 1 ch, tr2tog, 1 ch, 1 beaded ch, 1 ch and tr2tog), *1 dc into next ch sp working dc after beaded ch, 1 ch, miss tr2tog, 1 dc into next ch sp working dc before beaded ch, 3 ch, miss (tr2tog, 1 ch, 1 beaded ch, 1 ch, tr2tog and 1 ch), 1 dtr into next dc**, 3 ch, (miss (1 ch, tr2tog, 1 ch, 1 beaded ch, 1 ch and tr2tog), rep from * to end, ending last rep at **, turn.

Do NOT fasten off.

Edging

Thread beads onto yarn.

With RS facing, work around entire outer edge of Scarf as follows: 1 ch (does NOT count as st), work across top of last row as follows:

1 dc into dtr at end of last row and mark this dc, [3 dc into next ch sp, 1 dc into next dc, 1 dc into next ch sp, 1 dc into next dc, 3 dc into next ch sp] 3 times, 1 dc into 4th of 7 ch at beg of previous row and mark this dc, work down first row-end edge in dc, working a multiple of 6 dc plus 3 dc, 1 dc into foundation ch at base of first dc of foundation row and mark this dc, [3 dc into next ch sp, 1 dc into next ch at base of a dc of foundation row, 1 dc into next ch sp, 1 dc into next ch at base of a dc of foundation row, 3 dc into next ch sp] 3 times, 1 dc into ch at base of last dc of foundation row and mark this dc, work up other row-end edge in dc, working a multiple of 6 dc plus 3 dc, ss to first marked dc.

Next round: (RS) 1 ch (does NOT count as st), 1 dc into same place as ss at end of previous round – this is first marked corner dc, miss 1 dc, *(3 tr, 1 ch, 1 beaded ch, 1 ch, ss to top of last tr, and 3 tr) into next dc**, miss 2 dc, 1 dc into next dc, miss 2 dc, rep from * to end, noting that either side of marked corner dc only 1 dc will be missed (so that dc of this round is worked into corner dc and next tr group is only 1 st away from corner dc) and ending last rep at **, miss last dc, ss to first dc. Fasten off.

TO MAKE UP

Press very carefully following instructions on ball band, taking care not to damage the beads.

50 SKINNY SCARF AND HAT

■ *This scarf and hat combines a lurex yarn and matching coloured silver-lined beads but you could use contrasting or multi-coloured beads to give a completely different look.*
■ *Why not try wearing the scarf round your waist as a wide sash-style belt? This would jazz up a plain pair of trousers or a skirt and, if the belt carriers are wide enough, you could easily thread it through them.*

HAT

Thread beads onto yarn.

With 2.50 mm hook, make 140 ch and join with a ss to form a ring.

Round 1: (WS) 1 ch (does NOT count as st), 1 dc into first ch, *3 ch, miss 3 ch, 1 dc into next ch, 3 ch, miss 1 ch, 1 dc into next ch, 3 ch, miss 3 ch, 1 dc into next ch, rep from * to end, replacing dc at end of last rep with ss to first dc, **turn.** 14 patt reps.

Round 2: 1 ch (does NOT count as st), 1 dc into first dc, *1 ch, miss (3 ch and 1 dc), tr2tog into next ch sp, [1 ch, 1 beaded ch, 1 ch and tr2tog] 4 times into same ch sp, 1 ch, miss (1 dc and 3 ch), 1 dc into next dc, rep from * to end, replacing dc at end of last rep with ss to first dc, turn.

Round 3: 7 ch (counts as first dtr and 3 ch), miss (dc at base of 7 ch, 1ch, tr2tog, 1 ch, 1 beaded ch, 1 ch and tr2tog), *1 dc into next ch sp working dc after beaded ch, 3 ch, miss tr2tog, 1 dc into next ch sp working dc before beaded ch, 3 ch, miss (tr2tog, 1 ch, 1 beaded ch, 1 ch, tr2tog and 1 ch)**, 1 dtr into next dc, 3 ch, (miss (1 ch, tr2tog, 1 ch, 1 beaded ch, 1 ch and tr2tog), rep from * to end, ending last rep at **, ss to 4th of 7 ch at beg of round, turn.

Round 4: 1 ch (does NOT count as st), 1 dc into same place as ss at end of previous round, *1 ch, miss (3 ch and 1 dc), tr2tog into next ch sp, [1 ch, 1 beaded ch, 1 ch and tr2tog] 4 times into same ch sp, 1 ch, miss (1 dc and 3 ch), 1 dc into next dtr, rep from * to end, replacing dc at end of last rep with ss to first dc, turn.

Rounds 5 to 12: As rounds 3 and 4.

Round 13: 7 ch (counts as first dtr and 3 ch), miss (dc at base of 7 ch, 1 ch, tr2tog, 1 ch, 1 beaded ch, 1 ch and tr2tog), *1 dc into next ch sp working dc after beaded ch, 1 ch, miss tr2tog, 1 dc into next ch sp working dc before beaded ch, 3 ch, miss (tr2tog, 1 ch, 1 beaded ch, 1 ch, tr2tog and 1 ch)**, 1 dtr into next dc, 3 ch, (miss (1 ch, tr2tog, 1 ch, 1 beaded ch, 1 ch and tr2tog), rep from * to end, ending last rep at **, ss to 4th of 7 ch at beg of round, turn.

Round 14: (RS) 3 ch (counts as first tr), miss st at base of 3 ch, *3 tr into next ch sp, 1 tr into next dc, 1 tr into next ch sp, 1 tr into next dc, 3 tr into next ch sp**, 1 tr into next dtr, rep from * to end, ending last rep at **, ss to top of 3 ch at beg of round, do NOT turn. 140 sts. Without turning at ends of rounds (so that all foll rounds are RS rounds) cont as follows with unbeaded yarn:

Round 15: 3 ch (counts as first tr), miss st at base of 3 ch, 1 tr into each of next 7 tr, [tr2tog over next 2 tr, 1 tr into each of next 8 tr] 13 times, tr2tog over last 2 tr, ss to top of 3 ch at beg of round. 126 sts.

Round 16: 3 ch (counts as first tr), miss st at base of 3 ch, 1 tr into each of next 6 tr, [tr2tog over next 2 sts, 1 tr into each of next 7 tr] 13 times, tr2tog over last 2 sts, ss to top of 3 ch at beg of round. 112 sts.

Round 17: 3 ch (counts as first tr), miss st at base of 3 ch, 1 tr into each of next 5 tr, [tr2tog over next 2 sts, 1 tr into each of next 6 tr] 13 times, tr2tog over last 2 sts, ss to top of 3 ch

at beg of round. 98 sts.

Round 18: 3 ch (counts as first tr), miss st at base of 3 ch, 1 tr into each of next 4 tr, [tr2tog over next 2 sts, 1 tr into each of next 5 tr] 13 times, tr2tog over last 2 sts, ss to top of 3 ch at beg of round. 84 sts.

Round 19: 3 ch (counts as first tr), miss st at base of 3 ch, 1 tr into each of next 3 tr, [tr2tog over next 2 sts, 1 tr into each of next 4 tr] 13 times, tr2tog over last 2 sts, ss to top of 3 ch at beg of round. 70 sts.

Round 20: 3 ch (counts as first tr), miss st at base of 3 ch, 1 tr into each of next 2 tr, [tr2tog over next 2 sts, 1 tr into each of next 3 tr] 13 times, tr2tog over last 2 sts, ss to top of 3 ch at beg of round. 56 sts.

Round 21: 3 ch (counts as first tr), miss st at base of 3 ch, 1 tr into next tr, [tr2tog over next 2 sts, 1 tr into each of next 2 tr] 13 times, tr2tog over last 2 sts, ss to top of 3 ch at beg of round. 42 sts.

Round 22: 3 ch (counts as first tr), miss st at base of 3 ch, [tr2tog over next 2 sts, 1 tr into next tr] 13 times, tr2tog over last 2 sts, ss to top of 3 ch at beg of round. 28 sts.

Round 23: 3 ch (does NOT count as st), miss st at base of 3 ch, 1 tr into next st, [tr2tog over next 2 sts] 13 times, ss to top of first tr of round. 14 sts.

Round 24: 1 ch (does NOT count as st), [dc2tog over next 2 sts] 7 times, ss to first dc2tog, for top trim now make 11 ch, 1 dc into 2nd ch from hook, 1 dc into each of next 9 ch.
Fasten off.

TO MAKE UP

Press very carefully following instructions on ball band, taking care not to damage the beads.

Run a gathering thread around top of last round and pull up tight. Fasten off securely, catching free end of top trim inside centre.

Edging

Thread beads onto yarn.

With RS facing and using 2.50 mm hook, rejoin yarn to foundation ch edge of Hat, 1 ch (does NOT count as st), work 126 dc evenly around entire foundation ch edge (this is 9 dc for each rep), ss to first dc.

Next round: (RS) 1 ch (does NOT count as st), 1 dc into same place as ss at end of previous round, *miss 2 dc, (3 tr, 1 ch, 1 beaded ch, 1 ch, ss to top of last tr, and 3 tr) into next dc, miss 2 dc, 1 dc into next dc, rep from * to end, replacing dc at end of last rep with ss to first dc.
Fasten off.

■ *It would be easy to leave the beads off this pattern if you wanted to. Simply replace each beaded chain with a plain chain stitch.*
■ *Pressing this scarf or hat could damage the beads. If you feel it does need pressing, block it out by pinning into shape, covering it with a damp cloth and leaving it to dry naturally.*

Basic double crochet fabric in a twinkling lurex yarn is encrusted with beads to create the opulent look of these accessories. Use big faceted beads or mix metallic, faceted and glass beads of all shapes and sizes to make the belt.

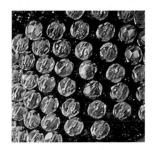

Cuff Bracelet and Sash Belt

EASY ★☆☆

MEASUREMENTS

CUFF BRACELET

Actual size
6 × 17 cm
2¼ × 6¾ in

SASH BELT (Actual size, excluding fringe)
6 × 125 cm
2¼ × 49¼ in

MATERIALS

Cuff Bracelet
- 1 × 25 g balls of Rowan Lurex Shimmer in Midnight 339
- 2.50 mm crochet hook
- 163 faceted crystal beads
- 4 buttons

Sash belt
- 2 × 50 g balls of Twilleys Goldfingering in Burnt Orange 64
- 2.50 mm crochet hook
- Approx 1,600 mixed beads

TENSION

26 sts and 30 rows to 10 cm (4 in) measured over beaded double crochet fabric using 2.50 mm hook. Change hook size if necessary to obtain this tension.

ABBREVIATIONS

See page 15.

For how to work with beads, see pages 16–17.

CUFF BRACELET

With 2.50 mm hook, make 16 ch.
Foundation row: (RS) 1 dc into 2nd ch from hook, 1 dc into each ch to end, turn. 15 dc.
Cont in patt as follows:
Row 1: (WS) 1 ch (does NOT count as st), 1 dc into first dc, *1 beaded dc into next dc, 1 dc into next dc, rep from * to end, turn.
Row 2: 1 ch (does NOT count as st), 1 dc into each dc to end, turn.
Row 3: 1 ch (does NOT count as st), 1 dc into first dc, *1 dc into next dc, 1 beaded dc into next dc, rep from * to last 2 dc, 1 dc into each of last 2 dc, turn.
Row 4: As row 2.
These 4 rows form patt.
Cont in patt for a further 46 rows, ending after patt row 2 and with a RS row.
Do NOT turn at end of last row.

CUFF BRACELET

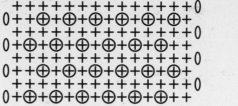

SASH BELT

Edging

Next round: (RS) 1 ch (does NOT count as st), work in dc evenly down row-end edge, across foundation ch edge, and up other row-end edge to beg of last row, 1 dc into first dc of last row of main piece, [3 ch (to make a buttonloop), miss 2 dc, 1 dc into each of next 2 dc] 3 times, 3 ch, miss 2 dc, ss to dc at beg of round.
Fasten off.
Attach buttons to correspond with buttonloops.

SASH BELT

With 2.50 mm hook, make 15 ch.
Foundation row: (RS) 1 dc into 2nd ch from hook, 1 dc into each ch to end, turn. 14 dc.
Cont in patt as follows:
Row 1: (WS) 1 ch (does NOT count as st), 1 dc into first dc, *1 beaded dc into next dc, 1 dc into next dc, rep from * to last dc, 1 dc into last dc, turn.
Row 2: 1 ch (does NOT count as st), 1 dc into each dc to end, turn.
Row 3: 1 ch (does NOT count as st), 1 dc into first dc, *1 dc into next dc, 1 beaded dc into next dc, rep from * to last dc, 1 dc into last dc, turn.
Row 4: As row 2.
These 4 rows form patt.
Cont in patt until Sash Belt measures 125 cm (49¼ in), ending with a RS row.
Fasten off.

Edging

With RS facing and using 2.50 mm hook, rejoin yarn to foundation ch at end of first row, 1 ch (does NOT count as st), now work 1 row of crab st (dc worked from left to right, instead of right to left) along one row-end edge to end of last row of main section, turn, with WS facing work across 14 sts of last row as follows: 1 dc into first dc, [31 ch, 1 dc into 2nd ch from hook, 1 dc into each of next 29 ch, 1 dc into each of next 4 dc of last row] 3 times, 31 ch, 1 dc into 2nd ch from hook, 1 dc into each of next 29 ch, 1 dc into last dc of last row, turn, now work 1 row of crab st (dc worked from left to right, instead of right to left) along other row-end edge to end of first row of main section, turn, with WS facing work across 14 sts of foundation ch edge as follows: 1 dc into first st, [31 ch, 1 dc into 2nd ch from hook, 1 dc into each of next 29 ch, 1 dc into each of next 4 sts of foundation ch edge] 3 times, 31 ch, 1 dc into 2nd ch from hook, 1 dc into each of next 29 ch, 1 dc into last st of foundation ch edge, ss to first dc.
Fasten off.

■ *This belt uses lots of different sorts of beads, from tiny metallic gold beads to quite large teardrop faceted glass beads. Mix together all the beads before you start and thread them onto the yarn randomly.*

■ *When making the bracelet, make sure the strip is long enough to fit around your wrist and adjust the length if you need to. But remember that it will stretch a little in wear.*

Wondrously simple to make, using just trebles, this big wrap is sure to get you noticed! Worked in an exquisite rainbow ribbon yarn, combining almost every colour imaginable, it's bound to match any and every outfit in your wardrobe.

Wrap

★ ☆ ☆

MEASUREMENTS

Actual size, excluding fringe
95 × 198 cm
37¹/₂ × 78 in

MATERIALS

- 16 × 50 g balls of Lion Brand Incredible in Purple Party 207
- 10.00 mm crochet hook

TENSION

8 sts and 4 rows to 10 cm (4 in) measured over treble fabric using 10.00 mm hook. Change hook size if necessary to obtain this tension.

ABBREVIATIONS

See page 15.

KEY
o *ch*
T *tr*

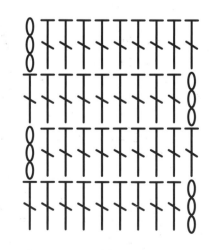

With 10.00 mm hook, make 78 ch.
Row 1: (RS) 1 tr into 4th ch from hook, 1 tr into each ch to end, turn. 76 sts.
Row 2: 3 ch (counts as first tr), miss tr at base of 3 ch, 1 tr into each tr to end, working last tr into top of 3 ch at beg of previous row, turn.
Last row forms tr fabric.
Cont in tr fabric until Wrap measures 198 cm (78 in).
Fasten off.

TO MAKE UP

Do NOT press.
Cut 60 cm (23¹/₂ in) lengths of yarn and knot one length through each st along foundation ch edge and along top of last row to form fringe.

- *There's no need to press your wrap once it's completed as this would spoil the full, rounded look of the stitches. But if the strands that make up the fringe become a little crumpled, simply mist them lightly with a water spray and let them hang free to dry naturally. This should remove any creases that may have formed.*
- *If you feel the very long fringe may be a bit too much for you, simply make it shorter. Or you could try knotting a few fancy beads onto some of the strands of the fringe to make it even more special.*
- *The amazing colours of this ribbon yarn turn simple trebles into something really special!*

Take a simple mesh stitch vest, add a glittering lurex yarn and a massive sprinkling of toning glittery beads and what do you get? This little vest top that will be just as at home with jeans or at the biggest of balls!

Beaded Vest

MEASUREMENTS

To fit bust

81	86	91	97	102	107	cm
32	34	36	38	40	42	in

Actual size, at underarm

85	89	95	99	105	109	cm
$33^{1}/_{2}$	35	$37^{1}/_{4}$	39	$41^{1}/_{4}$	43	in

Actual length

50	51	52	53	54	55	cm
$19^{3}/_{4}$	20	$20^{1}/_{2}$	$20^{3}/_{4}$	$21^{1}/_{4}$	$21^{1}/_{2}$	in

MATERIALS

- 3 (4: 4: 5: 6) × 50 g balls of Twilleys Goldfingering in turquoise 53
- 2.50 mm crochet hook
- Approx 9,160 (9,810: 10,650: 11,340: 12,220: 12,960) beads

TENSION

28 sts and 14 rows to 10 cm (4 in) measured over pattern using 2.50 mm hook. Change hook size if necessary to obtain this tension.

ABBREVIATIONS

tr2tog – *yoh and insert hook as indicated, yoh and draw loop through, yoh and draw through 2 loops, rep from * once more, yoh and draw through all 3 loops on hook.
See also page 15.

For how to work with beads, see pages 15–16.

BACK AND FRONT (Both alike)

With 2.50 mm hook, make 116 (122: 130: 136: 144: 150) ch and 1 beaded ch – 117 (123: 131: 137: 145: 151) ch in total.

Row 1: (RS) 1 tr into 5th ch from hook, *1 beaded ch, miss 1 ch, 1 tr into next ch, rep from * to end, turn. 115 (121: 129: 135: 143: 149) sts, 57 (60: 64: 67: 71: 74) beaded ch sps.

Cont in patt as follows:

Row 2: 3 ch (counts as first tr), miss tr at end of previous row, *1 beaded ch, miss 1 beaded ch, 1 tr into next tr, rep from * to end, working last tr into top of 3 ch at beg of previous row, turn. This row forms patt.

Work in patt for 1 row more.

Row 4: (WS) 3 ch (does NOT count as st), miss (1 tr and 1 beaded ch) at end of last row, 1 tr into next tr – 1 beaded ch sp decreased, patt to last 3 sts, tr2tog over last 3 sts, working first "leg" into next tr, missing beaded ch, and working 2nd "leg" into top of 3 ch at beg of previous row – 1 beaded ch sp decreased, turn. Working all decreases as set by last row, dec 1 beaded ch sp at each end of 3rd and every foll 3rd row until 49 (52: 56: 59: 63: 66) beaded ch sps rem.

Work 7 rows more.

Row 21: 3 ch (counts as first tr), 1 beaded ch, 1 tr into tr at end of previous row – 1 beaded ch sp increased, patt until tr has been worked into top of 3 ch at beg of previous row, 1 beaded ch, 1 tr into same place as last tr – 1 beaded ch sp increased, turn.

Working all increases as set by last row, inc 1 beaded ch sp at each end of 4th and every foll 4th row until there are 59 (62: 66: 69: 73: 76) beaded ch sps.

Cont straight until work measures 29 (30: 30: 31: 31: 32) cm, 11^1/$_2$ (11^3/$_4$: 11^3/$_4$: 12^1/$_4$: 12^1/$_4$: 12^1/$_2$) in.

Shape armholes

Next row: ss across first 6 (8: 8: 10: 10: 12) sts and into next tr, 3 ch (does NOT count as st), miss 1 beaded ch, 1 tr into next tr – 4 (5: 5: 6: 6: 7) beaded ch sps decreased, patt to last 9 (11: 11: 13: 13: 15) sts, tr2tog over next 3 sts, working first "leg" into next tr, missing beaded ch, and working 2nd "leg" into next tr and turn, leaving rem 6 (8: 8: 10: 10: 12) sts unworked – 4 (5: 5: 6: 6: 7) beaded ch sps decreased. 51 (52: 56: 57: 61: 62) beaded ch sps.

Working all decreases in same way as for side seam decreases, dec 1 beaded ch sp at each end of next 7 (7: 8: 8: 9: 9) rows. 75 (77: 81: 83: 87: 89) sts, 37 (38: 40: 41: 43: 44) beaded ch sps.

Shape neck

Next row: patt until 10th (10th: 11th: 11th: 12th: 12th) beaded ch has been worked, tr2tog over next 3 sts, working first "leg" into next tr, missing beaded ch, and working 2nd "leg" into next tr and turn, leaving rem sts unworked. 10 (10: 11: 11: 12: 12) beaded ch sps.

**Working all decreases in same way as for side seam decreases, dec 1 beaded ch sp at neck edge of next 7 rows. 7 (7: 9: 9: 11: 11) sts, 3 (3: 4: 4: 5: 5) beaded ch sps.

Cont straight until armhole measures 20 (20: 21: 21: 22: 22) cm, 7^3/$_4$ (7^3/$_4$: 8^1/$_4$: 8^1/$_4$: 8^1/$_2$: 8^1/$_2$) ins.

Fasten off.

Return to last complete row worked, miss centre 29 (31: 31: 33: 33: 35) sts, rejoin yarn to next tr and cont as follows:

Next row: 3 ch (does NOT count as st), miss st where yarn was rejoined and next beaded ch, 1 tr into next tr, patt to end, turn. 10 (10: 11: 11: 12: 12) beaded ch sps.

Complete to match first side from **.

TO MAKE UP

Press very carefully following instructions on ball band, taking care not to damage the beads. Join shoulder seams. Join side seams.

Hem Edging

With RS facing and using 2.50 mm hook, rejoin yarn at base of one side seam, 1 ch (does NOT count as st), work one round of dc evenly around entire lower edge, ending with ss to first dc, turn.

Round 1: (WS) 1 ch (does NOT count as st), 1 beaded dc into each dc to end, ss to first beaded dc, turn.

Round 2: 1 ch (does NOT count as st), 1 dc into each beaded dc to end, ss to first dc, turn.

Round 3: As round 1.

Fasten off.

Neck and Armhole Edgings

Work to match Hem Edging, rejoining yarn at a seam and missing dc as required whilst working round 2 to ensure Edging lies flat.

GLITTER

Shimmer and glitter in these sparkling designs, all worked
in fine lurex yarns. The metallic shades of gold, pewter,
bronze, copper and silver yarn give you all the glitter you
may need – but, if you want more, why not choose one of the
designs with sequins and beads? They are guaranteed to
make you a twinkling star on that big night.

*The big, bold gold sequins on this simple halter neck top,
worked in a smooth and silky yarn, make it a style to really get
you noticed. Not one for shrinking violets!*

Sequin Halter Neck

★★☆ INTERMEDIATE

MEASUREMENTS

To fit bust

81	86	91	97	102	107	cm
32	34	36	38	40	42	in

Actual size, at underarm

81	86	91	96	101	106	cm
32	34	36	$37^3/_4$	$39^3/_4$	$41^3/_4$	in

Actual length, from underarm

31	32	32	33	33	34	cm
$12^1/_4$	$12^1/_2$	$12^1/_2$	13	13	$13^1/_4$	in

MATERIALS

- 5 (5: 6: 7: 7: 8) × 50 g balls of Twilleys Silky in beige 101
- 2.00 mm crochet hook
- Approx 2,300 (2,500: 2,600: 2,900: 3,000: 3,300) large gold sequins

TENSION

32 sts and 20 rows to 10 cm (4 in) measured over pattern using 2.00 mm hook. Change hook size if necessary to obtain this tension.

ABBREVIATIONS

dc2tog – *insert hook as indicated, yoh and draw loop through, rep from * once more, yoh and draw through all 3 loops on hook; **dc3tog** – *insert hook as indicated, yoh and draw loop through, rep from * twice more, yoh and draw through all 4 loops on hook; **tr2tog** – *yoh and insert hook as indicated, yoh and draw loop through, yoh and draw through 2 loops, rep from * once more, yoh and draw through all 3 loops on hook; **tr3tog** – *yoh and insert hook as indicated, yoh and draw loop through, yoh and draw through 2 loops, rep from * twice more, yoh and draw through all 4 loops on hook.
See also page 15.

For how to work with sequins, see page 16–17.

BACK

With 2.00 mm hook, make 118 (126: 134: 142: 150: 158) ch.
Row 1: (RS) 1 dc into 2nd ch from hook, 1 dc into each ch to end, turn. 117 (125: 133: 141: 149: 157) sts.
Row 2: 1 ch (does NOT count as st), 1 dc into each dc to end, turn.
Rows 3 and 4: As row 2.
Cont in patt as follows:
Row 1: (RS) 3 ch (counts as first tr), miss dc at base of 3 ch, 1 tr into each dc to end, turn.
Row 2: 1 ch (does NOT count as st), 1 dc into each of first 2 tr, *1 sequinned dc into next tr, 1 dc into each of next 3 tr, rep from * to last 3 sts, 1 sequinned dc into next tr, 1 dc into each

- Make sure the sequins have the hole near one edge, not in the centre as otherwise they will not lie flat.
- Twilleys Silky is a very slippery yarn and the stitches can easily fall undone. Each time you put your work down, it's a good idea to slip the working loop onto a safety pin to make sure it does not unravel!
- This garment is designed to skim over the body and the actual finished size is about the same as the size it is to fit. If you want a tighter fitting garment, make a smaller size.
- When working the top edge shaping, remember not to place any sequins on the actual edge stitches of the rows as these edge sequins will get in the way when working the edgings.
- The sequins will tend to fold themselves out of position as this top is made. Once finished and in wear, gently smooth them all downwards to create the shimmery fish-scale effect.

of last 2 sts, working last dc into top of 3 ch at beg of previous row, turn.

Row 3: As row 1.

Row 4: 1 ch (does NOT count as st), 1 dc into each of first 4 tr, *1 sequinned dc into next tr, 1 dc into each of next 3 tr, rep from * to last 5 sts, 1 sequinned dc into next tr, 1 dc into each of last 4 sts, working last dc into top of 3 ch at beg of previous row, turn.

These 4 rows form patt.

Cont in patt for a further 2 rows, ending with a WS row.

Dec row: (RS) 3 ch (counts as first tr), miss dc at base of 3 ch, tr2tog over next 2 dc – 1 st decreased, 1 tr into each dc to last 3 dc, tr2tog over next 2 dc – 1 st decreased, 1 tr into last dc, turn.

Working all decreases as set by last row, dec 1 st at each end of every foll 4th row until 109 (117: 125: 133: 141: 149) sts rem.

Work 3 rows, ending with a WS row.

Inc row: (RS) 3 ch (counts as first tr), miss dc at base of 3 ch, 2 tr into next dc – 1 st increased, 1 tr into each dc to last 2 dc, 2 tr into next dc – 1 st increased, 1 tr into last dc, turn.

Working all increases as set by last row, inc 1 st at each end of every foll 4th row until there are 129 (137: 145: 153: 161: 169) sts, taking inc sts into patt.

Work a further 1 (3: 3: 5: 5: 7) rows, ending with a WS row.**

Fasten off.

FRONT

Work as given for Back to **.

Shape armholes

Next row: (RS) ss across and into 7th (9th: 11th: 13th: 15th: 17th) st, 3 ch (counts as first tr), miss dc at base of 3 ch, 1 tr into each dc to last 6 (8: 10: 12: 14: 16) dc and turn, leaving rem sts unworked. 117 (121: 125: 129: 133: 137) sts.

Next row: 1 ch (does NOT count as st), dc2tog over first 2 tr – 1 st decreased, patt to last 2 sts, dc2tog over last 2 sts – 1 st decreased, turn. 115 (119: 123: 127: 131: 135) sts.

Working all decreases as set by last row and Back side seam shaping, dec 1 st at each end of next 2 rows, ending with a WS row. 111 (115: 119: 123: 127: 131) sts.

Shape neck

Next row: (RS) 3 ch (counts as first tr), miss dc at base of 3 ch, tr2tog over next 2 dc – 1 st decreased, 1 tr into each of next 48 (50: 52: 54: 56: 58) dc, tr3tog over next 3 dc – 2 sts decreased, 1 tr into next dc and turn, leaving rem sts unworked. 52 (54: 56: 58: 60: 62) sts.

Next row: 1 ch (does NOT count as st), dc3tog over first 3 sts – 2 sts decreased, patt to last 2 sts, dc2tog over last 2 sts – 1 st decreased, turn. 49 (51: 53: 55: 57: 59) sts.

Working all decreases as now set, dec 2 sts at neck edge and 1 st at armhole edge of next 15 (15: 16: 17: 17: 18) rows, ending with a RS (RS: WS: RS: RS: WS) row. 4 (6: 5: 4: 6: 5) sts.

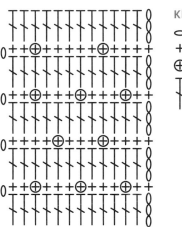

KEY

○ *ch*
+ *dc*
⊕ *sequinned dc*
⊤ *tr*

For 1st, 2nd, 4th and 5th sizes
Next row: (WS) 1 ch (does NOT count as st),
[dc2tog over next 2 sts] 2 (0: 2: 0) times,
[dc3tog over next 3 sts] 0 (2: 0: 2) times. 2 sts.

For 3rd and 4th sizes
Next row: (RS) 3 ch (does NOT count as st),
tr3tog over next 3 sts, 1 tr into last dc. 2 sts.

All sizes
Fasten off.
Return to last complete row worked, miss
centre dc, rejoin yarn to next dc with RS
facing, 3 ch (counts as first tr), miss dc at base
of 3 ch, tr3tog over next 3 dc – 2 sts decreased,
1 tr into each dc to last 3 dc, tr2tog over next
2 dc – 1 st decreased, 1 tr into last dc, turn. 52
(54: 56: 58: 60: 62) sts. Complete to match
first side, reversing shaping.

TO MAKE UP
Do NOT press.
Join side seams.

Front Neck Border
With RS facing and 2.00 mm hook, rejoin
yarn at left front fasten-off point, 1 ch (does
NOT count as st), work in dc down left front
slope, then up right front slope to right front
fasten-off point, working dc2tog either side of
base of V neck, turn.
Next row: 1 ch (does NOT count as st), 1 dc into
each dc to end, working dc2tog either side of
base of V neck, turn.
Rep last row twice more.
Fasten off.

Back and Armhole Borders and Ties
With 2.00 mm hook, make 150 ch, with RS
facing and starting at top of Front Neck
Border, work in dc evenly down right front
armhole edge, across top of Back, then up left
front armhole edge to top of other end of
Front Neck Border, 151 ch, turn.
Next row: (WS) 1 dc into 2nd ch from hook,
1 dc into each ch and dc to end, turn.
Next row: 1 ch (does NOT count as st), 1 dc into
each dc to end, turn.
Rep last row once more.
Fasten off.

Top off a simple dress with this neat bolero. Worked in a simple crunchy textured stitch, the edges are outlined with a row of bright and shiny sequins.

Bolero

MEASUREMENTS

To fit bust

81	86	91	97	102	107	cm
32	34	36	38	40	42	in

Actual size, at underarm

86	91	97	101	106	112	cm
33³/₄	35³/₄	38	39³/₄	41³/₄	44	in

Actual length

34	35	36	37	38	39	cm
13¹/₄	13³/₄	14	14¹/₂	15	15¹/₄	in

Actual sleeve

45	46	46	47	47	47	cm
17³/₄	18	18	18¹/₂	18¹/₂	18¹/₂	in

MATERIALS

- 7 (8: 9: 10: 11: 12) × 50 g balls of Twilleys Goldfingering in silver 5
- 2.50 mm crochet hook
- Approx 350 (370: 390: 400: 420: 430) large silver sequins

TENSION

32 sts and 20 rows to 10 cm (4 in) measured over pattern using 2.50 mm hook. Change hook size if necessary to obtain this tension.

ABBREVIATIONS

htr2tog – *yoh and insert hook as indicated, yoh and draw loop through, rep from * once more, yoh and draw through all 5 loops on hook; **htr3tog** – *yoh and insert hook as indicated, yoh and draw loop through, rep from * twice more, yoh and draw through all 7 loops on hook.
See also page 15.

For how to work with sequins, see pages 16–17.

BACK

With 2.50 mm hook, make 120 (129: 138: 144: 153: 162) ch.
Foundation row: (RS) (1 dc, 1 ch and 1 tr) into 3rd ch from hook, *miss 2 ch, (1 dc, 1 ch and 1 tr) into next ch, rep from * to last 3 ch, miss 2 ch, 1 htr into last ch, turn. 119 (128: 137: 143: 152: 161) sts, 39 (42: 45: 47: 50: 53) patt reps.
Cont in patt as follows:
Row 1: 2 ch (counts as first htr), miss first htr and next tr, *(1 dc, 1 ch and 1 tr) into next ch sp**, miss (1 dc and 1 tr), rep from * to end, ending last rep at **, miss 1 dc, 1 htr into top of turning ch, turn.
This row forms patt.
Keeping patt correct, cont as follows:
Work 2 rows, ending with a WS row.

- The crunchy texture of the simple stitch pattern used for this bolero contrasts well with the sleek shine of the sequins.
- Make sure you press the bolero pieces before you work the sequinned edging as, once the sequins are attached, you cannot press it as even a warm iron could melt them. If you need to press your completed bolero, take great care to cover the sequins with a cloth or simply block it out to shape.

- When working the sequinned edging, you may find it easier to thread all the sequins onto one ball of yarn. Use a plain ball for the first and last round of the edging, and the ball with the sequins on for the sequinned round. This will save repeatedly sliding all the sequins along the yarn to work the plain rounds.
- This bolero has large sequins that match the yarn colour – but you could use contrasting coloured sequins, smaller ones or even fancy beads.

Next row: (RS) 2 ch (counts as first htr), 1 htr into htr at base of 2 ch – 1 st increased, miss next tr, *(1 dc, 1 ch and 1 tr) into next ch sp**, miss (1 dc and 1 tr), rep from * to end, ending last rep at **, miss 1 dc, 2 htr into top of turning ch – 1 st increased, turn.

Next row: 2 ch (counts as first htr), 1 htr into htr at base of 2 ch, 1 ch – 2 sts increased, 1 htr into next htr, miss next 1 tr, *(1 dc, 1 ch and 1 tr) into next ch sp**, miss (1 dc and 1 tr), rep from * to end, ending last rep at **, miss 1 dc, 1 htr into next htr, 1 ch, 2 htr into top of turning ch – 2 sts increased, turn. 125 (134: 143: 149: 158: 167) sts. Patt 1 row across all sts, working first and last patt rep into ch sp between htr. 41 (44: 47: 49: 52: 55) patt reps. (1 patt rep increased at each edge over 3 rows.)

Working all increases as now set, cont as follows:
Work 2 rows.
Inc 1 patt rep at each edge over next 3 rows.
Rep last 5 rows once more. 137 (146: 155: 161: 170: 179) sts, 45 (48: 51: 53: 56: 59) patt reps.
Cont straight until Back measures 12 (13: 13: 14: 14: 15) cm, 4³/4 (5: 5: 5¹/2: 5¹/2: 6) in, ending with a WS row.

Shape armholes
Next row: (RS) ss across first 6 sts and into 7th st, 2 ch (counts as first htr) – 2 patt reps decreased, patt to last 7 sts, 1 htr into next st and turn, leaving rem 6 sts unworked - 2 patt reps decreased. 125 (134: 143: 149: 158: 167) sts, 41 (44: 47: 49: 52: 55) patt reps.

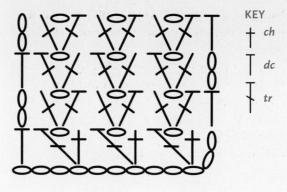

KEY
† ch
T dc
T tr

Next row: 2 ch (does NOT count as st), htr2tog over next 2 sts, 1 htr into next st – 2 sts decreased, patt to last 5 sts, miss next dc, 1 htr into next tr, htr3tog over next 3 sts – 2 sts decreased, turn.

Next row: 2 ch (does NOT count as st), 1 htr into next st – 1 st decreased, patt to last 2 sts, htr2tog over next htr and htr2tog – 1 st decreased. 119 (128: 137: 143: 152: 161) sts.
Patt 1 row across all sts. 39 (42: 45: 47: 50: 53) patt reps. (1 patt rep decreased at each edge over 3 rows.)
Rep last 3 rows 2 (3: 4: 5: 6: 6) times more. 107 (110: 113: 113: 116: 125) sts, 35 (36: 37: 37: 38: 41) patt reps.
Cont straight until armholes measure 20 (20: 21: 21: 22: 22) cm, 7³/4 (7³/4: 8¹/4: 8¹/4: 8¹/2: 8¹/2) in, ending with a WS row.
Fasten off, placing markers either side of centre 55 (58: 61: 61: 64: 61) sts to denote back neck.

LEFT FRONT
With 2.50 mm hook, make 60 (63: 69: 72: 75: 81) ch.
Work foundation row as given for Back. 59 (62: 68: 71: 74: 80) sts, 19 (20: 22: 23: 24: 26) patt reps.
Cont in patt as given for Back as follows:
Work 3 rows, ending with a WS row.
Working all shaping as given for Back, cont as follows:
Inc 1 patt rep at side seam edge of next 3 rows.
Work 2 rows.

Rep last 5 rows once more, then first 3 rows again. 68 (71: 77: 80: 83: 89) sts, 22 (23: 25: 26: 27: 29) patt reps.
Cont straight until Left Front matches Back to start of armhole shaping, ending with a WS row.

Shape armhole
Dec 6 sts, 2 patt reps at beg of next row. 62 (65: 71: 74: 77: 83) sts, 20 (21: 23: 24: 25: 27) patt reps.

Shape front slope
Dec 1 patt rep at armhole and at front slope edge over next 3 rows, 3 (4: 5: 6: 7: 7) times. 44 (41: 41: 38: 35: 41) sts, 14 (13: 13: 12: 11: 13) patt reps.
Work 1 row, then dec 1 patt rep at front slope edge over next 3 rows.
Rep last 4 rows 5 (4: 4: 3: 2: 2) times more. 26 (26: 26: 26: 26: 32) sts, 8 (8: 8: 8: 8: 10) patt reps.
Cont straight until Left Front matches Back to shoulder, ending with a WS row.
Fasten off.

RIGHT FRONT
Work to match Left Front, reversing shapings.

SLEEVES
With 2.50 mm hook, make 78 (78: 81: 81: 84: 84) ch.
Work foundation row as given for Back. 77 (77: 80: 80: 83: 83) sts, 25 (25: 26: 26: 27: 27) patt reps.

Cont in patt as given for Back as follows:
Work 7 rows, ending with a WS row.
Working all shaping as given for Back, cont as follows:
Inc 1 patt rep at each end over next 3 rows.
Work 13 (13: 13: 13: 11: 11) rows.
Rep last 16 (16: 16: 16: 14: 14) rows 3 (3: 3: 3: 4: 4) times more, then first 3 of these rows again. 107 (107: 110: 110: 119: 119) sts, 35 (35: 36: 36: 39: 39) patt reps.
Cont straight until Sleeve measures 43 (44: 44: 45: 45: 45) cm, 17 (17^1/$_4$: 17^1/$_4$: 17^3/$_4$: 17^3/$_4$: 17^3/$_4$) in, ending with a RS row.

Shape top
Working all shaping as given for Back, dec 6 sts, 2 patt reps at each end of next row. 95 (95: 98:

98: 107: 107) sts, 31 (31: 32: 32: 35: 35) patt reps.
Dec 1 patt rep at each end over next 3 rows, 8 (8: 8: 8: 9: 9) times. 47 (47: 50: 50: 53: 53) sts, 15 (15: 16: 16: 17: 17) patt reps.
Fasten off.

TO MAKE UP
Press carefully following instructions on ball band.
Join shoulder seams. Join side seams. Join sleeve seams. Sew Sleeves into armholes.

Edging
Thread sequins onto yarn.
With 2.50 mm hook, rejoin yarn at base of one side seam, 1 ch (does NOT count as st), work 1 round of dc evenly around entire hem, front opening and neck edges, ending with ss to first dc and ensuring an even number of sts are worked, **turn.**
Next round: (WS) 1 ch (does NOT count as st), *1 dc into next dc, 1 sequinned dc into next dc, rep from * to end, ss to first dc, turn.
Next round: 1 ch (does NOT count as st), 1 dc into each st to end, ss to first dc.
Fasten off.
Work Edging around lower edge of Sleeves in same way, rejoining yarn at base of sleeve seam.

Combining metallic shades of silver, bronze and gold, this loose fitting top is made up of lots of clever motifs. The motifs are joined as they are made, so there's no sewing up afterwards.

Kimono Top

MEASUREMENTS

One size, to fit bust	**Actual size**
86–107 cm	120 cm
34–42 in	47¼ in

Actual length	**Actual sleeve**
30 cm	30 cm
11¾ in	11¾ in

MATERIALS

- Twilleys Goldfingering: 2 × 50 g balls in colour A (silver 5), 2 × 50 g balls in colour B (bronze 52), and 3 × 50 g balls in colour C (gold 2)
- 2.50 mm crochet hook

TENSION

Motif measures 10 cm (4 in) square on 2.50 mm hook. Change hook size if necessary to obtain this tension.

ABBREVIATIONS

picot – 3 ch, ss to top of dc just worked; ttr - triple treble. *See also page 15.*

MOTIF

With 2.50 mm hook and first colour (either A or B), make 4 ch and join with a ss to form a ring.

Round 1: (RS) 1 ch (does NOT count as st), 1 dc into ring, [4 ch, 1 ttr into ring, 4 ch, 1 dc into ring] 4 times, replacing dc at end of last rep with ss to first dc.
Break off first colour and join in second colour (either B or A) to same place as ss.
Round 2: 11 ch (counts as first dtr and 7 ch), miss (first dc and 4 ch), *1 dc into next ttr, 7 ch**, miss 4 ch, 1 dtr into next dc, 7 ch, miss 4 ch, rep from * to end, ending last rep at **, ss to 4th of 11 ch at beg of round.
Round 3: 4 ch (counts as first dtr), 2 dtr into st at base of 4 ch, *1 ch, 1 dc into next ch sp, 1 ch, (3 ttr, 2 ch and 3 ttr) into next dc, 1 ch, 1 dc into next ch sp, 1 ch**, 3 dtr into next dtr, rep from * to end, ending last rep at **, ss to top of 4 ch at beg of round.
Round 4: 1 ch (does NOT count as st), 1 dc into same place as ss at end of previous round, 1 dc into each of next 2 dtr, *1 dc into next ch sp, 1 dc into next dc, 1 dc into next ch sp, 1 dc into each of next 2 ttr, miss next ttr, 3 dc into next ch sp, miss next ttr, 1 dc into each of next 2 ttr, 1 dc into next ch sp, 1 dc into next dc, 1 dc into next ch sp**, 1 dc into each of next 3 dtr, rep from * to end, ending last rep at **, ss to first dc. 64 sts.
Break off second colour and join in C to 2nd dc at beg of round.

					A	B	A	B	A	B				
	A	B	A	B	A	B	A	B	A	B	A	B		
	B	A	B	A	B	A	B	A	B	A	B	A		
	A	B	A	B	A	X B	A	Y B	A	B	A	B		
	B	A	B	A	B	A	B	A	B	A	B	A		
					B	A	B	A	B	A				

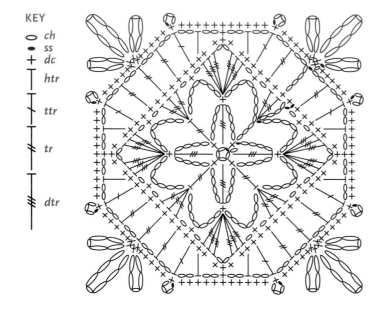

KEY

○ ch
● ss
+ dc
├ htr
╪ ttr
╪ tr
╪ dtr

Round 5: 6 ch (counts as first dtr and 2 ch), miss 1 dc, 1 dtr into next dc, *2 ch, miss 1 dc, 1 tr into next dc, 2 ch, miss 1 dc, 1 htr into next dc, 2 ch, miss 1 dc, 1 dc into next dc, 2 ch, miss 1 dc, 1 htr into next dc, 2 ch, miss 1 dc, 1 tr into next dc**, [2 ch, miss 1 dc, 1 dtr into next dc] 3 times, rep from * to end, ending last rep at **, 2 ch, miss 1 dc, 1 dtr into next dc, 2 ch, miss 1 dc, ss to 4th of 6 ch at beg of round.

Round 6: 1 ch (does NOT count as st), (1 dc, 5 ch, 1 dc, 7 ch, 1 dc, 5 ch and 1 dc) into same place as ss at end of previous round, *2 dc into next ch sp, 1 dc into next dtr, 2 dc into next ch sp, 1 dc into next tr, 1 picot, [2 dc into next ch sp, 1 dc into next st] 4 times, 1 picot, 2 dc into next ch sp, 1 dc into next dtr, 2 dc

into next ch sp**, (1 dc, 5 ch, 1 dc, 7 ch, 1 dc, 5 ch and 1 dc) into next dtr, rep from * to end, ending last rep at **, ss to first dc.
Fasten off.
Motif should be 10 cm (4 in) square – adjust hook size now if required.

In each corner of Motif, there are three ch loops – a central 7-ch loop with a 5-ch loop each side, and along sides of Motif between these groups of ch loops there are 2 picots of 3 ch. Whilst working Round 6, join Motifs at corners, by replacing corner (7 ch) with (3 ch, 1 ss into corner 7-ch loop of adjacent Motif, 3 ch), and at picots, by replacing picot (3 ch) with (1 ch, 1 ss into picot of adjacent Motif, 1 ch).

TOP

Following diagram, make and join 60 Motifs to form shape shown. On diagram, letter indicates colour to use for round 1 – either A or B. If using A for round 1, use B for rounds 2 to 4, and vice versa. Use C for rounds 5 and 6 of **ALL** Motifs. Join side and underarm seams whilst joining Motifs as indicated by arrows, and do NOT join Motifs between X and Y to form neck opening (join first "shoulder" Motifs at the picots but NOT at the corners nearest the neck edge).

TO MAKE UP

Press carefully following instructions on ball band.

Encrusted with faceted beads, this stylish cardigan will ensure you sparkle! Worked in a combination of double crochet and trebles, it's the stunning beads that give this design its impact.

Beaded Cardigan

ADVANCED ★★★

MEASUREMENTS

To fit bust

81	86	91	97	102	107	cm
32	34	36	38	40	42	in

Actual size, at underarm

87	92	96	101	105	110	cm
34¹/₄	36¹/₄	37³/₄	39³/₄	41¹/₄	43¹/₄	in

Actual length

57	58	59	60	61	62	cm
22¹/₂	22³/₄	23¹/₄	23¹/₂	24	24¹/₄	in

Actual sleeve

45	45	46	46	46	47	cm
17³/₄	17³/₄	18	18	18	18¹/₂	in

MATERIALS

- 24 (25: 26: 28: 29: 30) × 100 g balls of Rowan Lurex Shimmer in Copper 330
- 2.50 mm crochet hook
- Approx 1,800 (1,900: 2,000: 2,100: 2,200: 2,300) × crystal beads
- 5 buttons

TENSION

26 sts and 18 rows to 10 cm (4 in) measured over pattern using 2.50 mm hook. Change hook size if necessary to obtain this tension.

ABBREVIATIONS

dc2tog – *insert hook as indicated, yoh and draw loop through, rep from * once more, yoh and draw through all 3 loops on hook; **tr2tog** – *yoh and insert hook as indicated, yoh and draw loop through, yoh and draw through 2 loops, rep from * once more, yoh and draw through all 3 loops on hook.
See also page 15.

For how to work with beads, see pages 16–17.

BACK

With 2.50 mm hook, make 111 (117: 123: 129: 135: 141) ch.
Foundation row: (RS) 1 tr into 4th ch from hook, 1 tr into each ch to end, turn. 109 (115: 121: 127: 133: 139) sts.
Cont in patt as follows:
Row 1: (WS) 1 ch (does NOT count as st), 1 dc into each of first 6 (3: 6: 3: 6: 3) tr, 1 beaded dc into next tr, *1 dc into each of next 5 tr, 1 beaded dc into next tr, rep from * to last 6 (3: 6: 3: 6: 3) sts, 1 dc into each of last 6 (3: 6: 3: 6: 3) sts, working last dc into top of 3 ch at beg of previous row, turn.
Row 2: 3 ch (counts as first tr), miss dc at base of 3 ch, 1 tr into each dc to end, turn.

■ Rowan Lurex Shimmer is quite a delicate yarn and could be easily damaged by repeatedly slipping too many beads along it. To avoid the risk of this happening, thread the beads onto the yarn in batches of about 200 beads. Once these beads have been used up, break the yarn and thread on some more.

■ When working the shaping, don't place a bead on an edge stitch of a row as this will make it difficult to sew up the seam.

Row 3: 1 ch (does NOT count as st), 1 dc into each tr to end, working last dc into top of 3 ch at beg of previous row, turn.

Row 4: As row 2.

Row 5: 1 ch (does NOT count as st), 1 dc into each of first 3 (6: 3: 6: 3: 6) tr, 1 beaded dc into next tr, *1 dc into each of next 5 tr, 1 beaded dc into next tr, rep from * to last 3 (6: 3: 6: 3: 6) sts, 1 dc into each of last 3 (6: 3: 6: 3: 6) sts, working last dc into top of 3 ch at beg of previous row, turn.

Rows 6 and 7: As rows 2 and 3.

Row 8: 3 ch (does NOT count as st), miss dc at base of 3 ch, 1 tr into next dc – 1 st decreased, 1 tr into each dc to last 2 dc, tr2tog over last 2 dc – 1 st decreased, turn. 107 (113: 119: 125: 131: 137) sts.

These 8 rows form patt and start side seam shaping.

Keeping patt correct, cont as follows:

Work 2 rows, ending with a RS row.

Next row: (WS) 1 ch (does NOT count as st), dc2tog over first 2 tr – 1 st decreased, patt to last 2 sts, dc2tog over last 2 sts (second of these is the 3 ch at beg of previous row) – 1 st decreased, turn. 105 (111: 117: 123: 129: 135) sts.

Working all shaping as now set, dec 1 st at each end of 3rd and every foll 3rd row until 95 (101: 107: 113: 119: 125) sts rem.

Work 1 row, ending with a WS row.

Work mock belt

Row 1: (RS) 1 ch (does NOT count as st), working into back loops only of previous row, 1 dc into each dc to end, turn.

Row 2: 1 ch (does NOT count as st), 1 dc into each dc to end, turn.

Row 3: 1 ch (does NOT count as st), 1 dc into each dc to end, turn.

Row 4: (WS) 1 ch (does NOT count as st), 1 dc into each of first 2 dc, *1 beaded dc into next dc, 1 dc into each of next 2 dc, rep from * to end, turn.

Rows 5 to 10: As rows 3 and 4, 3 times.

Rows 11 to 13: As row 2.

Row 14: 1 ch (does NOT count as st), working into front loops only of previous row, 1 dc into each dc to end, turn.

These 14 rows complete mock belt.

Now cont in patt as follows:

Next row: (RS) 3 ch (counts as first tr), 1 tr into dc at base of 3 ch – 1 st increased, 1 tr into each dc to last dc, 2 tr into last dc – 1 st increased, turn. 97 (103: 109: 115: 121: 127) sts.

Next row: 1 ch (does NOT count as st), 1 dc into each of first 6 (3: 6: 3: 6: 3) tr, 1 beaded dc into next tr, *1 dc into each of next 5 tr, 1 beaded dc into next tr, rep from * to last 6 (3: 6: 3: 6: 3) sts, 1 dc into each of last 6 (3: 6: 3: 6: 3) sts, working last dc into top of 3 ch at beg of previous row, turn.

Next row: 3 ch (counts as first tr), miss dc at base of 3 ch, 1 tr into each dc to end, turn.

Next row: 1 ch (does NOT count as st), 2 dc

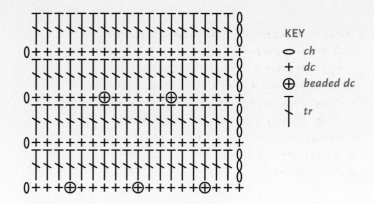

KEY
○ ch
+ dc
⊕ beaded dc
⊤ tr

into first tr – 1 st increased, 1 dc into each tr to last st, 2 dc into top of 3 ch at beg of previous row – 1 st increased, turn. 99 (105: 111: 117: 123: 129) sts.

Last 4 rows set position of patt and increases. Keeping patt correct as now set and working all increases as now set, inc 1 st at each end of every foll 3rd row until there are 113 (119: 125: 131: 137: 143) sts, taking inc sts into patt.

Cont straight until Back measures 37 (38: 38: 39: 39: 40) cm, 14¹/₂ (15: 15: 15¹/₄: 15¹/₄: 15³/₄) in, ending with a RS row.

Shape armholes

Next row: (WS) ss across first 4 (5: 5: 6: 6: 7) tr and into next tr, 1 ch (does NOT count as st), 1 dc into same tr as last ss - 4 (5: 5: 6: 6: 7) sts decreased, patt to last 4 (5: 5: 6: 6: 7) sts and turn, leaving rem 4 (5: 5: 6: 6: 7) sts unworked - 4 (5: 5: 6: 6: 7) sts decreased. 105 (109: 115: 119: 125: 129) sts.

Working all decreases in same way as for side seam decreases, dec 1 st at each end of next 9 (10: 12: 13: 15: 16) rows. 87 (89: 91: 93: 95: 97) sts.

Cont straight until armholes measure 20 (20: 21: 21: 22: 22) cm, 7³/₄ (7³/₄: 8¹/₄: 8¹/₄: 8¹/₂: 8¹/₂) in, ending with a WS row.

Fasten off, placing markers either side of centre 39 (41: 41: 43: 43: 43) sts to denote back neck.

LEFT FRONT

With 2.50 mm hook, make 61 (64: 67: 70: 73: 76) ch.

Foundation row: (RS) 1 tr into 4th ch from hook, 1 tr into each ch to end, turn. 59 (62: 65: 68: 71: 74) sts. Cont in patt as follows:

Row 1: (WS) 1 ch (does NOT count as st), 1 dc into each of first 4 tr, 1 beaded dc into next tr, *1 dc into each of next 5 tr, 1 beaded dc into next tr, rep from * to last 6 (3: 6: 3: 6: 3) sts, 1 dc into each of last 6 (3: 6: 3: 6: 3) sts, working last dc into top of 3 ch at beg of previous row, turn.

Row 2: 3 ch (counts as first tr), miss dc at base of 3 ch, 1 tr into each dc to end, turn.

Row 3: 1 ch (does NOT count as st), 1 dc into each tr to end, working last dc into top of 3 ch at beg of previous row, turn.

Row 4: As row 2.

Row 5: 1 ch (does NOT count as st), 1 dc into first tr, 1 beaded dc into next tr, *1 dc into each of next 5 tr, 1 beaded dc into next tr, rep from * to last 3 (6: 3: 6: 3: 6) sts, 1 dc into each of last 3 (6: 3: 6: 3: 6) sts, working last dc into top of 3 ch at beg of previous row, turn.

Rows 6 and 7: As rows 2 and 3.

Row 8: 3 ch (does NOT count as st), miss dc at base of 3 ch, 1 tr into next dc – 1 st decreased, 1 tr into each dc to end, turn. 58 (61: 64: 67: 70: 73) sts.

These 8 rows form patt and start side seam shaping.

Keeping patt correct, cont as follows:

Working all shaping as set by Back, dec 1 st at side seam edge of every foll 3rd row until 52 (55: 58: 61: 64: 67) sts rem.

Work 1 row, ending with a WS row.

Work mock belt

Row 1: (RS) 1 ch (does NOT count as st), working into back loops only of previous row, 1 dc into each dc to end, turn.

Row 2: 1 ch (does NOT count as st), 1 dc into each dc to end, turn.

Row 3: 1 ch (does NOT count as st), 1 dc into each dc to end, turn.

Row 4: (WS) 1 ch (does NOT count as st), 1 dc into first dc, *1 beaded dc into next dc, 1 dc into each of next 2 dc, rep from * to end, turn.

Rows 5 to 10: As rows 3 and 4, 3 times.

Rows 11 to 13: As row 2.

Row 14: 1 ch (does NOT count as st), working into front loops only of previous row, 1 dc into each dc to end, turn.

These 14 rows complete mock belt.

Now cont in patt as follows:

Next row: (RS) 3 ch (counts as first tr), 1 tr into dc at base of 3 ch – 1 st increased, 1 tr into each dc to end, turn. 53 (56: 59: 62: 65: 68) sts.

Next row: 1 ch (does NOT count as st), 1 dc into each of first 4 tr, 1 beaded dc into next tr, *1 dc into each of next 5 tr, 1 beaded dc into next tr, rep from * to last 6 (3: 6: 3: 6: 3) sts, 1 dc into each of last 6 (3: 6: 3: 6: 3) sts, working last dc into top of 3 ch at beg of previous row, turn.

Next row: 3 ch (counts as first tr), miss dc at base of 3 ch, 1 tr into each dc to end, turn.

Next row: 1 ch (does NOT count as st), 1 dc into each tr to last st, 2 dc into top of 3 ch at beg of previous row – 1 st increased, turn. 54 (57: 60: 63: 66: 69) sts.

Last 4 rows set position of patt and increases. Keeping patt correct as now set and working all increases as now set, inc 1 st at side seam edge of every foll 3rd row until there are 61 (64: 67: 70: 73: 76) sts, taking inc sts into patt. Cont straight until Left Front matches Back to start of armhole shaping, ending with a RS row.

Shape armhole

Working all shaping in same way as given for Back, dec 4 (5: 5: 6: 6: 7) sts at end of next row. 57 (59: 62: 64: 67: 69) sts.

Dec 1 st at armhole edge of next 9 (10: 12: 13: 15: 16) rows. 48 (49: 50: 51: 52: 53) sts.

Cont straight until 14 (14: 14: 16: 16: 16) rows less have been worked than on Back to shoulder fasten-off, ending with a WS row.

Shape neck

Next row: (RS) 3 ch (counts as first tr), miss dc at base of 3 ch, 1 tr into each of next 34 (34: 35: 36: 37: 38) dc and turn, leaving rem 13 (14: 14: 14: 14: 14) sts unworked.

Dec 1 st at neck edge on next 10 rows, then on 1 (1: 1: 2: 2: 2) alt rows. 24 (24: 25: 25: 26: 27) sts.

Work 1 row, ending with a WS row.

Fasten off.

Mark positions for 5 buttons along Left Front opening edge – lowest button level with row 7 of mock belt, top button 2 cm, 3/4 in, below neck shaping, and rem 3 buttons evenly spaced between.

RIGHT FRONT

With 2.50 mm hook, make 61 (64: 67: 70: 73: 76) ch.

Foundation row: (RS) 1 tr into 4th ch from hook, 1 tr into each ch to end, turn. 59 (62: 65: 68: 71: 74) sts.

Cont in patt as follows:

Row 1: (WS) 1 ch (does NOT count as st), 1 dc into each of first 6 (3: 6: 3: 6: 3) tr, 1 beaded dc into next tr, *1 dc into each of next 5 tr, 1 beaded dc into next tr, rep from * to last 4 sts, 1 dc into each of last 4 sts, working last dc into top of 3 ch at beg of previous row, turn.

Row 2: 3 ch (counts as first tr), miss dc at base of 3 ch, 1 tr into each dc to end, turn.

Row 3: 1 ch (does NOT count as st), 1 dc into each tr to end, working last dc into top of 3 ch at beg of previous row, turn.

Row 4: As row 2.

Row 5: 1 ch (does NOT count as st), 1 dc into each of first 3 (6: 3: 6: 3: 6) tr, 1 beaded dc into next tr, *1 dc into each of next 5 tr, 1 beaded dc into next tr, rep from * to last st, 1 dc into top of 3 ch at beg of previous row, turn.

Rows 6 and 7: As rows 2 and 3.

Row 8: 3 ch (counts as first tr), miss dc at base of 3 ch, 1 tr into each dc to last 2 dc, tr2tog over last 2 dc – 1 st decreased, turn. 58 (61: 64: 67: 70: 73) sts.

These 8 rows form patt and start side seam shaping.

Keeping patt correct, cont as follows:

Working all shaping as set by Back, dec 1 st at side seam edge of 3rd and every foll 3rd row until 52 (55: 58: 61: 64: 67) sts rem.

Work 1 row, ending with a WS row.

Work mock belt

Row 1: (RS) 1 ch (does NOT count as st), working into back loops only of previous row, 1 dc into each dc to end, turn.

Row 2: 1 ch (does NOT count as st), 1 dc into each dc to end, turn.

Row 3: 1 ch (does NOT count as st), 1 dc into each dc to end, turn.

Row 4: (WS) 1 ch (does NOT count as st), 1 dc into each of first 2 dc, *1 beaded dc into next dc, 1 dc into each of next 2 dc, rep from * to last 2 dc, 1 beaded dc into next dc, 1 dc into last dc, turn.

Rows 5 and 6: As rows 3 and 4.

Row 7: 1 ch (does NOT count as st), 1 dc into each of first 3 dc, 2 ch, miss 2 dc (to make a buttonhole), 1 dc into each dc to end, turn.

Row 8: 1 ch (does NOT count as st), 1 dc into each of first 2 dc, *1 beaded dc into next dc, 1 dc into each of next 2 dc, rep from * to last 5 sts, 2 dc into next ch sp, 1 dc into next dc, 1 beaded dc into next dc, 1 dc into last dc, turn.

Rows 9 and 10: As rows 3 and 4.

Rows 11 to 13: As row 2.

Row 14: 1 ch (does NOT count as st), working into front loops only of previous row, 1 dc into each dc to end, turn.

These 14 rows complete mock belt.

Now cont in patt as follows:

Next row: (RS) 3 ch (counts as first tr), miss dc at base of 3 ch, 1 tr into each dc to last dc, 2 tr into last dc – 1 st increased, turn. 53 (56: 59: 62: 65: 68) sts.

Next row: 1 ch (does NOT count as st), 1 dc into each of first 6 (3: 6: 3: 6: 3) tr, 1 beaded dc into next tr, *1 dc into each of next 5 tr, 1 beaded dc into next tr, rep from * to last 4 sts, 1 dc into each of last 4 sts, working last dc into top of 3 ch at beg of previous row, turn.

Next row: 3 ch (counts as first tr), miss dc at base of 3 ch, 1 tr into each dc to end, turn.

Next row: 1 ch (does NOT count as st), 2 dc into first tr – 1 st increased, 1 dc into each tr to end, working last dc into top of 3 ch at beg of previous row, turn. 54 (57: 60: 63: 66: 69) sts.

Last 4 rows set position of patt and increases.

Complete to match Left Front, reversing shapings and working a further 4 buttonholes to correspond with positions marked for buttons as follows:

Buttonhole row: (WS) 1 ch (does NOT count as st), patt to last 5 sts, 2 ch, miss 2 tr (to make a buttonhole – on next row work 2 tr into this ch sp), patt rem 3 sts, turn.

SLEEVES

With 2.50 mm hook, make 58 (58: 60: 62: 62: 64) ch.

Row 1: (RS) 1 dc into 2nd ch from hook, 1 dc into each ch to end, turn. 57 (57: 59: 61: 61: 63) sts.

Row 2: 1 ch (does NOT count as st), 1 dc into each dc to end, turn.

Row 3: 1 ch (does NOT count as st), 1 dc into each dc to end, turn.

Row 4: (WS) 1 ch (does NOT count as st), 1 dc into each of first 1 (1: 2: 3: 3: 1) dc, *1 beaded dc into next dc, 1 dc into each of next 2 dc, rep from * to last 2 (2: 3: 4: 4: 2) dc, 1 beaded dc into next dc, 1 dc into each of last 1 (1: 2: 3: 3: 1) dc, turn.

Rows 5 to 10: As rows 3 and 4, 3 times.

Rows 11 to 13: As row 2.

Row 14: 1 ch (does NOT count as st), working into front loops only of previous row, 1 dc into each dc to end, turn.

These 14 rows complete mock cuff.

Cont in patt as follows:

Row 1: (RS) 3 ch (counts as first tr), 1 tr into dc at base of 3 ch – 1 st increased, 1 tr into each dc to last dc, 2 tr into last dc – 1 st increased, turn. 59 (59: 61: 63: 63: 65) sts.

Row 2: 1 ch (does NOT count as st), 1 dc into each of first 5 (5: 6: 1: 1: 2) tr, 1 beaded dc into next tr, *1 dc into each of next 5 tr, 1 beaded dc into next tr, rep from * to last 5 (5: 6: 1: 1: 2) sts, 1 dc into each of last 5 (5: 6: 1: 1: 2) sts, working last dc into top of 3 ch at beg of previous row, turn.

Row 3: 3 ch (counts as first tr), miss dc at base of 3 ch, 1 tr into each dc to end, turn.

Row 4: 1 ch (does NOT count as st), 1 dc into each tr to end, working last dc into top of 3 ch at beg of previous row, turn.

Row 5: As row 1. 61 (61: 63: 65: 65: 67) sts.

Row 6: 1 ch (does NOT count as st), 1 dc into each of first 3 (3: 4: 5: 5: 6) tr, 1 beaded dc into next tr, *1 dc into each of next 5 tr, 1 beaded dc

into next tr, rep from * to last 3 (3: 4: 5: 5: 6) sts, 1 dc into each of last 3 (3: 4: 5: 5: 6) sts, working last dc into top of 3 ch at beg of previous row, turn.

Rows 7 and 8: As rows 3 and 4.

These 8 rows form patt and start sleeve shaping. Cont in patt, shaping sides by inc 1 st at each end of next and every foll 4th row to 67 (73: 75: 77: 83: 83) sts, then on every foll 6th row until there are 83 (85: 87: 89: 91: 93) sts, taking inc sts into patt.

Cont straight until Sleeve measures 45 (45: 46: 46: 46: 47) cm, 17³/4 (17³/4: 18: 18: 18: 18¹/2) in, ending with a RS row.

Shape top

Working all shaping as given for Back, dec 4 (5: 5: 6: 6: 7) sts at each end of next row. 75 (75: 77: 77: 79: 79) sts.

Dec 1 st at each end of every row until 27 sts rem. Fasten off.

TO MAKE UP

Do NOT press.
Join shoulder seams.

COLLAR

With RS facing and using 2.50 mm hook, starting and ending on 5th sts in from front opening edges, work around neck edge as follows: 1 ch (does NOT count as st), 23 (23: 23: 25: 25: 25) dc up right side of neck, 38 (41: 41: 43: 43: 43) dc across back neck, then 23 (23: 23: 25: 25: 25) dc down left side of neck, turn. 84 (87: 87: 93: 93: 93) sts.

Row 1: (WS) 1 ch (does NOT count as st), 1 dc into first dc, 1 beaded dc into next dc, *1 dc into each of next 2 dc, 1 beaded dc into next dc, rep from * to last dc, 1 dc into last dc, turn.

Row 2: 1 ch (does NOT count as st), 1 dc into each of first 6 (7: 7: 8: 8: 8) dc, dc2tog over next 2 dc, *1 dc into each of next 12 (12: 12: 13: 13: 13) dc, dc2tog over next 2 dc, rep from * to last 6 (8: 8: 8: 8: 8) dc, 1 dc into each of last 6 (8: 8: 8: 8: 8) dc, turn. 78 (81: 81: 87: 87: 87) sts.

Row 3: As row 1.

Row 4: 1 ch (does NOT count as st), 1 dc into each of first 5 (4: 4: 5: 5: 5) dc, dc2tog over next 2 dc, *1 dc into each of next 11 (12: 12: 13: 13: 13) dc, dc2tog over next 2 dc, rep from * to last 6 (5: 5: 5: 5: 5) dc, 1 dc into each of last 6 (5: 5: 5: 5: 5) dc, turn. 72 (75: 75: 81: 81: 81) sts.

Row 5: As row 1.

Row 6: 1 ch (does NOT count as st), 1 dc into each of first 5 (4: 4: 4: 4: 4) dc, dc2tog over next 2 dc, *1 dc into each of next 10 (11: 11: 12: 12: 12) dc, dc2tog over next 2 dc, rep from * to last 5 (4: 4: 5: 5: 5) dc, 1 dc into each of last 5 (4: 4: 5: 5: 5) dc, turn. 66 (69: 69: 75: 75: 75) sts.

Row 7: As row 1.

Row 8: 1 ch (does NOT count as st), 1 dc into each dc to end, turn.

Row 9: As row 8.

Fasten off.

Join side seams. Join Sleeve seams. Sew Sleeves into armholes.

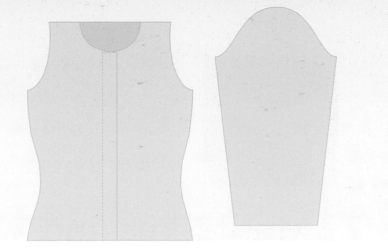

Hem and Lower Front Opening Edging

With **WS** facing and 2.50 mm hook, rejoin yarn to right front opening edge just below row 1 of mock belt, 1 ch (does NOT count as st), work 1 row of dc evenly down right front opening edge, across entire hem, then up left front opening edge to just below row 1 of mock belt, working 3 dc into hem corner points.
Fasten off.

Collar and Upper Front Opening Edging

With **WS** facing and 2.50 mm hook, rejoin yarn to left front opening edge level with row 14 of mock belt, 1 ch (does NOT count as st), work 1 row of dc evenly up left front opening edge, around neck corner point and along to base of Collar, working 3 dc into neck corner point, **turn**, work one row of crab st (dc worked from left to right, instead of right to left) around entire outer edge of Collar, **turn**, work 1 row of dc evenly from base of collar across to right front opening edge, then down right front opening edge to level with row 14 of mock belt, working 3 dc into neck corner point.
Fasten off.

Mock Belt Edging

With RS facing and 2.50 mm hook, rejoin yarn to left front opening edge level with row 14 of mock belt, 1 ch (does NOT count as st), working into rem free loops of row 13 of mock belt work 1 row of crab st (dc worked from left to right, instead of right to left) evenly around body to right front opening edge, then down right front opening edge of mock belt to loops left free by row 1 of mock belt, then work back around body working into this row of free loops to left front opening edge, then up left front opening edge to row 14 of mock belt.
Fasten off.

Upper Mock Cuff Edging

With RS facing and 2.50 mm hook, rejoin yarn to sleeve seam level with row 14 of mock cuff, 1 ch (does NOT count as st), working into rem free loops of row 13 of mock cuff work 1 round of crab st (dc worked from left to right, instead of right to left) evenly around sleeve, ending with ss to first dc.
Fasten off.

Lower Mock Cuff Edging

With RS facing and 2.50 mm hook, rejoin yarn to base of sleeve seam, 1 ch (does NOT count as st), work 1 round of crab st (dc worked from left to right, instead of right to left) evenly around foundation ch edge, ending with ss to first dc.
Fasten off.
Sew on buttons.

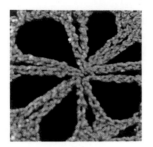

Simple triangular motifs make up this easy-to-wear skirt and wrap. A little time-consuming to make but it's worth the effort as you will want to wear it again and again. Team them with a little top or a cosy sweater – either way you'll still sparkle.

Motif Skirt and Wrap

INTERMEDIATE

MEASUREMENTS

SKIRT

To fit hip

81	86–91	96–102	107	112–117	cm
32	34–36	38–40	42	44–46	in

Actual size

88	96	104	112	120	cm
$34^1/_2$	$37^3/_4$	41	44	$47^1/_4$	in

Actual length (from below Waist Casing)

64	64	64	64	64	cm
25	25	25	25	25	in

WRAP

Actual size

58 × 186 cm
$22^3/_4 \times 73^1/_4$ in

MATERIALS

- Rowan Lurex Shimmer in Pewter 333: 13 (14:15:16:17) × 25 g balls for Skirt, 22 × 25 g balls for Wrap
- 2.50 mm crochet hook
- Waist length of 2.5 cm (1 in) wide elastic for Skirt

TENSION

Motif measures 8 cm ($3^1/_8$ in) along all 3 sides on 2.50 mm hook. Change hook size if necessary to obtain this tension.

ABBREVIATIONS

See page 15.

MOTIF

With 2.50 mm hook, make 4 ch and join with a ss to form a ring.

Round 1: (RS) 5 ch (counts as first tr and 2 ch), [1 tr into ring, 2 ch] 5 times, ss to 3rd of 5 ch at beg of round.

Round 2: 3 ch (counts as first tr), 3 tr into first ch sp, [1 tr into next tr, 3 tr into next ch sp] 5 times, ss to top of 3 ch at beg of round. 24 sts.

Round 3: 1 ch (does NOT count as st), 1 dc into first st, *5 ch, miss 1 tr, 1 dc into next tr, 5 ch, miss 2 tr, (3 tr, 11 ch and 3 tr) into next tr, 5 ch, miss 2 tr, 1 dc into next tr, rep from * twice more, replacing dc at end of last rep with ss to first dc.

Fasten off.

Motif is a triangle. In each corner there is an 11-ch sp, and along sides there are a further three 5-ch sps. Join Motifs whilst working Round 3 at corners, by replacing corner (11 ch) with (5 ch, 1 ss into corner 11-ch sp of adjacent Motif, 5 ch), and at side ch sps, by replacing (5 ch) with (2 ch, 1 ss into corresponding ch sp of adjacent Motif, 2 ch).

- The triangular motifs used here can be joined to form hexagons – so why not make a matching bag? Simply join two sets of six motifs to form two hexagons, join these hexagons and add a simple strip of crochet to form a strap.
- Make the skirt longer or shorter by simply adding or leaving out a band of 2 rows of motifs at the lower edge. But remember this will mean the amount of yarn you need will change!

- When working the waist casing of the skirt, make sure that the edge will stretch over your hips once it is sewn in place.
- These garments have a simple scalloped edging added afterwards – but you could leave them plain or work a lacy edging if you preferred.

SKIRT

Following diagram, make and join 198 (216: 234: 252: 270) Motifs to form shape shown. On diagram, work the shaded section the number of times shown so that there are 11 (12: 13: 14: 15) Motifs across each row. Join centre back seam whilst joining Motifs by joining end of strip, matching A to A, B to B, C to C, etc, so that final joined Motif section forms a tube.

Hem Edging

With RS facing and using 2.50 mm hook, rejoin yarn to lower edge at any joining point between Motifs, 1 ch (does NOT count as st), work across base of each Motif as follows:
*1 dc into joining point, 4 dc into next ch sp, 1 dc into each of next 3 tr, 3 dc into each of next 3 ch sps, 1 dc into each of next 3 tr, 4 dc into next ch sp, rep from * to end, ss to first dc. 264 (288: 312: 336: 360) sts.***
Next round: (RS) 1 ch (does NOT count as st), 1 dc into st at base of 1 ch, *miss 2 dc, 6 tr into next dc, miss 2 dc, 1 dc into next dc, rep from * to end, replacing dc at end of last rep with ss to first dc.
Fasten off.

TO MAKE UP
Press carefully following instructions on ball band.

Waist Casing
Work around upper edge of Motif tube as given for Hem Edging to ***.
Next round: (RS) 3 ch (counts as first tr), miss st at base of 3 ch, 1 tr into each st to end, ss to top of 3 ch at beg of round.
Rep last round 6 times more.
Fasten off.
Fold Waist Casing in half to inside and stitch in place, leaving an opening. Thread elastic through casing and join ends. Sew casing opening closed.

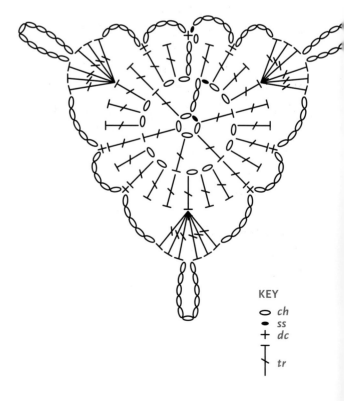

KEY

○ *ch*
● *ss*
+ *dc*
┬ *tr*

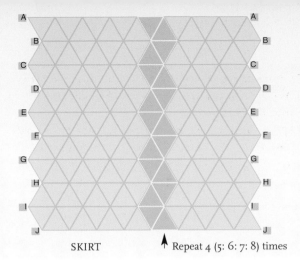

SKIRT   ↑ Repeat 4 (5: 6: 7: 8) times

WRAP

WRAP

Following diagram, make and join 360 Motifs
to form shape shown. On diagram, work the
shaded section 7 times, then work unshaded
section so that there are 22 Motifs along each
long edge.

Edging

With RS facing and using 2.50 mm hook,
rejoin yarn to one long edge at any joining
point between Motifs, 1 ch (does NOT count as
st), work across edge of each Motif as follows:
*1 dc into joining point, 4 dc into next ch sp,
1 dc into each of next 3 tr, 3 dc into each of next
3 ch sps, 1 dc into each of next 3 tr, 1 dc into
next ch sp, rep from * to end, ss to first dc.
Next round: (RS) 1 ch (does NOT count as st),
1 dc into st at base of 1 ch, *miss 2 dc, 6 tr into
next dc, miss 2 dc, 1 dc into next dc, rep from
* to end, replacing dc at end of last rep with
ss to first dc.
Fasten off.

TO MAKE UP

Press carefully following instructions on
ball band.

TENDER IS THE NIGHT

Soft and gentle shades of pinks, purples and greys will
accentuate your femininity for that special night out. Choose
from the softest of pinks for an evening dress, or combine
pearls and opalescent yarn for a useful bag. Use a simple
but soft yarn for the little shoulder capelet, or iridescent
beads for a neat little shoulder purse. Whichever design you
choose you'll look simply beautiful!

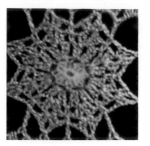

Combine simple lacy stitches and circular motifs with shimmering lurex and the softest of kid mohair yarns. Add a sprinkling of toning beads and create this stunning dress that will definitely have them falling at your feet.

Evening Dress

★★★ ADVANCED

MEASUREMENTS

To fit bust

81–86	91–97	102–107	cm
32–34	36–38	40–42	in

Actual size, at underarm

84	95	105	cm
33	37^1/$_2$	41^1/$_4$	in

Actual length, from shoulder (approx)

117	118	119	cm
46	46^1/$_2$	47	in

MATERIALS

- 40 (43: 46) × 25 g balls of Rowan Lurex Shimmer in Gleam 336 (M)
- Rowan Kidsilk Haze: 3 (3: 4) × 25 g balls in Dewberry 600 (A – dark mauve), and 3 (4: 4) × 25 g balls in Grace 580 (B – pale pink)
- 2.50 mm crochet hook
- Beads: approx 2000 (2300: 2500) × small round beads, and approx 430 (480: 540) × teardrop glass beads

TENSION

Large Motif measures 18 cm (7 in) in diameter, Small Motif measures 9 cm (3^1/$_2$ in) in diameter, both on 2.50 mm hook. 6 pattern repeats to 10.5 cm (4^1/$_8$ in) and 10 rows to 10 cm (4 in) measured over pattern using 2.50 mm hook. Change hook size if necessary to obtain this tension.

For how to work with beads, see page 15.

ABBREVIATIONS

tr2tog=*yoh and insert hook as indicated, yoh and draw loop through, yoh and draw through 2 loops, rep from * once more, yoh and draw through all 3 loops on hook. *See also pages 16–17.*

LARGE MOTIF

Thread 8 round beads onto A.

With 2.50 mm hook and A, make 4 ch and join with a ss to form a ring.

Round 1: (RS) 3 ch (counts as first tr), 15 tr into ring, ss to top of 3 ch at beg of round, turn. 16 sts.

Round 2: 1 ch (does NOT count as st), 1 beaded dc into first st, *2 ch, miss 1 tr, 1 beaded dc into next tr, rep from * to end, replacing beaded dc at end of last rep with ss to first dc, turn. 8 ch sps. Fasten off A and join M to first ch sp.

Round 3: 3 ch (counts as first tr), (1 tr, 1 ch and 2 tr) into same ch sp, *1 ch**, (2 tr, 1 ch and 2 tr) into next ch sp, rep from * to end, ending last rep at **, ss to top of 3 ch at beg of round. 48 sts.

Round 4: ss across and into first ch sp, 3 ch (counts as first tr), (1 tr, 1 ch and 2 tr) into same ch sp, *1 ch, 1 dc into next ch sp, 1 ch**, (2 tr, 1 ch and 2 tr) into next ch sp, rep from * to end, ending last rep at **, ss to top of 3 ch at beg of round.

■ *When working the hem flounce of this design, don't worry that the rounds don't appear to lie flat – they are not supposed to! They should form an undulating wave of mohair and beaded mesh.*

■ *You could make this dress longer or shorter by simply working more or less rows in the skirt section. But remember this will affect the amount of yarn you need!*

Round 5: ss across and into first ch sp, 3 ch (counts as first tr), (1 tr, 2 ch and 2 tr) into same ch sp, *2 ch, 1 dc into next dc, 2 ch**, miss the next ch sp, (2 tr, 2 ch and 2 tr) into next ch sp, rep from * to end, ending last rep at **, ss to top of 3 ch at beg of round. Fasten off M.

Motif is currently an 8-pointed star shape, with a 2-ch sp at end of each point.

Thread 32 round beads onto yarn B.

Join in B to one 2-ch sp at end of one point and cont as follows:-

Round 6: 1 ch (does NOT count as st), 1 dc into ch sp where yarn was rejoined, *8 ch, 1 dc into ch sp at end of next point, rep from * to end, replacing dc at end of last rep with ss to first dc. 8 ch sps.

Round 7: 3 ch (counts as first tr), miss dc at base of 3 ch, *(1 tr, 1 beaded ch, [3 tr, 1 beaded ch] 3 times and 1 tr) into next ch sp**, 1 tr into next dc, rep from to end, ending last rep at **, ss to top of 3 ch at beg of round.

Round 8: 1 ch (does NOT count as st), 1 dc into each of first 2 sts, *miss beaded ch ensuring bead is left sitting on RS of work**, 1 dc into each of next 3 tr, rep from * to end, ending last rep at **, 1 dc into last tr, ss to first dc. 96 sts. Fasten off B.

- *The weight of the skirt section of this dress means it could easily "drop" if left hanging up. So it is a good idea to store it laid flat.*
- *This dress is supposed to be figure hugging and should appear a little small before it's put on. Once on the body though, it should gently ease out to hug and flatter the figure.*

Join in M to 1 dc around outer edge and cont as follows:-

Round 9: 1 ch (does NOT count as st), 1 dc into dc where yarn was rejoined, *2 ch, miss 1 dc, 1 dc into next dc, rep from * to end, replacing dc at end of last rep with ss to first dc. 48 ch sps.

Round 10: ss into first ch sp, 3 ch (counts as first tr), (1 tr, 1 ch and 2 tr) into same ch sp, *1 ch, miss 1 ch sp**, (2 tr, 1 ch and 2 tr) into next ch sp, rep from * to end, ending last rep at **, ss to top of 3 ch at beg of round.

Round 11: as round 4.

Round 12: ss across and into first ch sp, 3 ch (counts as first tr), (1 tr, 3 ch and 2 tr) into same ch sp, *2 ch, 1 dc into next dc, 2 ch**, (2 tr, 3 ch and 2 tr) into next ch sp, rep from * to end, ending last rep at **, ss to top of 3 ch at beg of round.
Fasten off.

Motif is a 24-pointed star shape, with a 3-ch sp at end of each point, and a dc at the base of each V between each point. Join Motifs at relevant points whilst working round 12 by replacing (3 ch) with (1 ch, ss into ch sp of adjacent Motif, 1 ch).

SMALL MOTIF

Work as given for Basic Large Motif to end of round 4 but using yarn B in place of yarn A.

Round 5: ss across and into first ch sp, 3 ch (counts as first tr), (1 tr, 3 ch and 2 tr) into same ch sp, *2 ch, 1 dc into next dc, 2 ch**, (2 tr, 3 ch and 2 tr) into next ch sp, rep from * to end, ending last rep at **, ss to top of 3 ch at beg of round. Fasten off.

Motif is an 8-pointed star shape, with a 3-ch sp at end of each point, and a dc at the base of each V between each point. Join Motifs at relevant points whilst working round 5 by replacing (3 ch) with (1 ch, ss into ch sp of adjacent Motif, 1 ch).

UPPER MOTIF BAND

Make and join 8 (9: 10) Small Motifs to form a loop as follows:- leave top 2 points free, join side 2 points to side 2 points of adjacent Motif, leave lower 2 points free, and join other 2 side points to next Motif.

BODICE

With 2.50 mm hook and RS facing, rejoin M to a dc between 2 free points across top of one Motif of Upper Motif Band, ***6 ch (counts as 1 tr and 3 ch), working around top of Upper Motif Band, cont as follows: *1 dc into next free point of same Motif, 3 ch, 1 dtr into next dc at base of V between point just worked into and point joined to next Motif, 3 ch, 1 qtr into joined point of this Motif and next Motif, 3 ch, 1 dtr into next dc at base of V between point just worked into and first free point of next Motif, 3 ch, 1 dc into first free point of same Motif, 3 ch**, 1 tr into dc between 2 free points across top of this Motif, 3 ch rep from * to end, ending last rep at **, ss to 3rd of 6 ch at beg of round, turn. 48 (54: 60) ch sps.

Next round: ss across and into first ch sp, 3 ch (counts as first tr), (1 tr, 2 ch and 2 tr) into same ch sp, (2 tr, 2 ch and 2 tr) into each ch sp to end, ss to top of 3 ch at beg of round, turn. Cont in patt as follows:-

Round 1: (RS) ss across and into first ch sp, 3 ch (counts as first tr), (1 tr, 2 ch and 2 tr) into same ch sp, (2 tr, 2 ch and 2 tr) into next ch sp, rep from * to end, ss to top of 3 ch at beg of round, turn. 48 (54: 60) patt reps.
This round forms patt.****
Work in patt for a further 9 rounds, ending after a WS round.

Divide for armholes

Fasten off.

Mark points 12 (13½: 15) patt reps either side of beg/end of last round – these are underarm points. (On 2nd size, underarm point falls on a ch sp at the centre of a patt rep, and on other 2 sizes, underarm point falls between 2 patt reps.) There should be 24 (27: 30) patt reps between markers – set that includes beg/end of rounds will form back, other set will form front.

Shape front

With RS facing and counting from left underarm point, miss 0 (underarm ch sp: 0) and next 3 (4: 5) ch sps, attach M to centre of next ch sp and cont as follows:-

Row 1: (RS) 3 ch (counts as first tr), 1 tr into same ch sp, [(2 tr, 2 ch and 2 tr) into next ch sp] 16 (16: 18) times, 2 tr into next ch sp, turn.

Row 2: 3 ch (does NOT count as st), patt until (2 tr, 2 ch and 1 tr) have been worked into last 2-ch sp, tr2tog working first "leg" into same ch sp as last tr and second "leg" into top of 3 ch at beg of previous row, turn.

Row 3: 3 ch (does NOT count as st), (1 tr, 1 ch and 2 tr) into first 2-ch sp, patt until one 2-ch sp remains at end of row, (2 tr and 1 ch) into last 2-ch sp, tr2tog working first "leg" into same ch sp as last tr and second "leg" into first tr of previous row, turn.

Row 4: 3 ch (counts as first tr), 1 tr into first (1-ch) sp, patt until the one 1-ch sp remains at end of row, 1 tr into this ch sp, 1 tr into first tr of previous row, turn.

Row 5: 3 ch (counts as first tr), miss last 4 tr of previous row, patt until (2 tr, 2 ch and 2 tr) have been worked into last 2-ch sp, miss 3 tr, 1 tr into top of 3 ch at beg of previous row, turn.

Row 6: 3 ch (counts as first tr), (2 tr, 2 ch and 2 tr) into each 2-ch sp to end, 1 tr into top of 3 ch at beg of previous row. 14 (14: 16) patt reps.

Shape neck

Row 1: 3 ch (counts as first tr), (2 tr, 2 ch and 2 tr) into each of first three 2-ch sps, 2 tr into next ch sp and turn, leaving rem sts unworked.

Row 2: 3 ch (does NOT count as st), miss 4 tr, (2 tr, 2 ch and 2 tr) into each of next three 2-ch sps, 1 tr into top of 3 ch at beg of previous row, turn.

Row 3: 3 ch (counts as first tr), (2 tr, 2 ch and 2 tr) into each of first two 2-ch sps, (2 tr and 1 ch) into last 2-ch sp, tr2tog working first "leg" into same ch sp as last tr and second "leg" into first tr of previous row, turn.

Row 4: 3 ch (counts as first tr), 1 tr into first (1-ch) sp, (2 tr, 2 ch and 2 tr) into each of next two 2-ch sps, 1 tr into top of 3 ch at beg of previous row, turn.

Row 5: 3 ch (counts as first tr), (2 tr, 2 ch and 2 tr) into each of next two 2-ch sps, miss 3 tr, 1 tr into top of 3 ch at beg of previous row, turn.

Row 6: 3 ch (counts as first tr), (2 tr, 2 ch and 2 tr) into each 2-ch sp to end, 1 tr into top of 3 ch at beg of previous row. 2 patt reps.

Rep row 6 until armhole measures 20 (21: 22) cm, $7^3/_4$ ($8^1/_4$: $8^1/_2$) ins. Fasten off.

Return to last complete row worked before neck shaping, miss centre 6 (6: 8) ch sps, attach yarn to centre of next ch sp, 3 ch (counts as first tr), 1 tr into same ch sp, patt to end. Complete second side to match first, reversing shapings.

Shape back

Return to last complete round worked before start of front shaping and, counting from right underarm point, miss 0 (underarm ch sp: 0) and next 3 (4: 5) ch sps, attach M to centre of next ch sp and complete back exactly as for front. (There should be 6 (9: 10) ch sps left free at each underarm point.)

LOWER MOTIF BAND

Make and join 16 (18: 20) Large Motifs to form a loop as follows:- leave top 5 points free, join side 5 points to side 5 points of adjacent Motif, leave lower 9 points free, and join other 5 side points to next Motif.

SKIRT

With 2.50 mm hook and RS facing, rejoin M to the dc directly below centre back between 2 free points across lower edge of one Motif of Upper Motif Band and work around lower edge of Motif Band as for Bodice from *** to ****.

Work in patt for a further 5 rounds, ending after a WS round.

Next round: ss across and into first ch sp, 3 ch (counts as first tr), (1 tr, 2 ch, 2 tr, 2 ch and 2 tr) into same ch sp, *[(2 tr, 2 ch and 2 tr) into next ch sp] 5 times**, (2 tr, 2 ch, 2 tr, 2 ch and 2 tr) into next ch sp, rep from * to end, ending last rep at **, ss to top of 3 ch at beg of round, turn.

Next round: ss across and into first ch sp, 3 ch (counts as first tr), (1 tr, 2 ch and 2 tr) into same ch sp, (2 tr, 2 ch and 2 tr) into each ch sp to end, ss to top of 3 ch at beg of round, turn. 56 (63: 70) patt reps.

Work 8 rounds.

Next round: ss across and into first ch sp, 3 ch (counts as first tr), (1 tr, 2 ch, 2 tr, 2 ch and

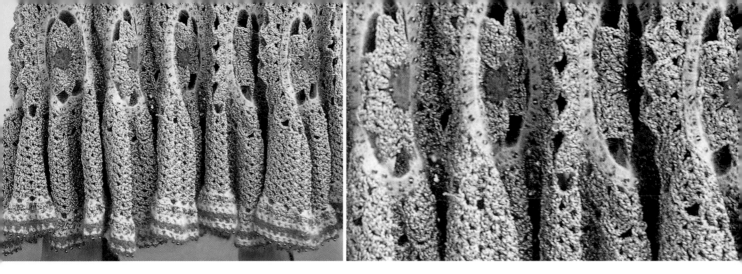

2 tr) into same ch sp, *[(2 tr, 2 ch and 2 tr) into next ch sp] 6 times**, (2 tr, 2 ch, 2 tr, 2 ch and 2 tr) into next ch sp, rep from * to end, ending last rep at **ss to top of 3 ch at beg of round, turn.

Next round: ss across and into first ch sp, 3 ch (counts as first tr), (1 tr, 2 ch and 2 tr) into same ch sp, (2 tr, 2 ch and 2 tr) into each ch sp to end, ss to top of 3 ch at beg of round, turn. 64 (72: 80) patt reps.
Work 8 rounds.

Next round: ss across and into first ch sp, 3 ch (counts as first tr), (1 tr, 2 ch, 2 tr, 2 ch and 2 tr) into same ch sp, *[(2 tr, 2 ch and 2 tr) into next ch sp] 7 times**, miss 4 tr, (2 tr, 2 ch, 2 tr, 2 ch and 2 tr) into next ch sp, rep from * to end, ending last rep at **, ss to top of 3 ch at beg of round, turn.

Next round: ss across and into first ch sp, 3 ch (counts as first tr), (1 tr, 2 ch and 2 tr) into same ch sp, (2 tr, 2 ch and 2 tr) into each ch sp to end, ss to top of 3 ch at beg of round, turn. 72 (81: 90) patt reps.
Work 8 rounds.

Next round: ss across and into first ch sp, 3 ch (counts as first tr), (1 tr, 2 ch and 2 tr) into same ch sp, *[(2 tr, 2 ch and 2 tr) into next ch sp] 8 times**, (2 tr, 2 ch, 2 tr, 2 ch and 2 tr) into next ch sp, rep from * to end, ending last rep at **, ss to top of 3 ch at beg of round, turn.

Next round: ss across and into first ch sp, 3 ch (counts as first tr), (1 tr, 2 ch and 2 tr) into

same ch sp, (2 tr, 2 ch and 2 tr) into each ch sp to end, ss to top of 3 ch at beg of round, turn. 80 (90: 100) patt reps.
Work 8 rounds.

Join Skirt to Lower Motif Band

Next round: ss across and into first ch sp, 1 ch (does NOT count as st), 1 dc into same ch sp, 3 ch, 1 dc into centre free point of one Motif around upper edge of Lower Motif Band, *3 ch, 1 dc into next ch sp of Skirt, 4 ch, 1 dc into next free point of same Motif, 4 ch, 1 dc into next ch sp of Skirt, 5 ch, 1 dc into next free point of same Motif, 5 ch, 1 dc into next ch sp of Skirt, 5 ch, 1 dc into first free point of next Motif, 5 ch, 1 dc into next ch sp of Skirt, 4 ch, 1 dc into next free point of same Motif, 4 ch**, 1 dc into next ch sp of Skirt, 3 ch, 1 dc into next (centre) free point of same Motif, rep from * to end, ending last rep at **, ss to first dc. Fasten off.

SKIRT HEM FLOUNCE

With 2.50 mm hook and RS facing, rejoin M to ch sp of first free point of any motif around lower edge of Lower Motif Band and work around lower edge of Lower Motif Band as follows: 1 ch (does NOT count as st), 1 dc into same free point as where yarn was joined, *3 ch, 1 tr into next dc at base of V after point just worked into, 3 ch, 1 dc into next free point (or 1 tr into pair of joined points), rep from * to end, replacing dc at end of last rep with ss

to first dc, turn. 320 (360: 400) ch sps.
Round 1: (WS) ss across and into first ch sp,
3 ch (counts as first tr), (1 tr, 2 ch and 2 tr) into
same ch sp, (2 tr, 2 ch and 2 tr) into each ch sp
to end, ss to top of 3 ch at beg of round, turn.
320 (360: 400) patt reps.
Work in patt for a further 8 rounds.
Thread 320 (360: 400) teardrop beads onto B.
Join in yarn B to first ch sp.
Round 10: (RS) using B, 3 ch (counts as first
tr), (1 tr, 2 ch and 2 tr) into same ch sp, *1
beaded ch**, (2 tr, 2 ch and 2 tr) into next ch
sp, rep from * to end, ending last rep at **,
ss to top of 3 ch at beg of round, turn.
Round 11: Using M, 1 ch (does NOT count as st),
1 dc into last ch sp of previous round placing this
dc so that it sits after bead, *3 ch, 1 dc into next 2-
ch sp, 3 ch**, (1 dc, 3 ch and 1 dc) into next
beaded ch sp ensuring bead sits between the
2 dc, rep from * to end, ending last rep at **,
1 dc into next beaded ch sp placing this dc before
the beaded ch, 2 ch, 1 dc into first dc, turn.
Round 12: Using M, 1 ch (does NOT count as
st), 1 dc into ch sp partly formed by 2 ch at end
of previous round, *3 ch, 1 dc into next ch sp,
rep from * until dc has been worked into last
3-ch sp, 2 ch, 1 dc into first dc, turn. Break off
M.
Rounds 13 and 14: Using B, as round 12.
Join in A.
Rounds 15 and 16: Using A, as round 12.
Round 17: Using B, as round 12.
Break off B.

Thread 960 (1080: 1200) round beads onto A.
Round 18: Using A, 1 ch (does NOT count as
st), 1 dc into ch sp partly formed by 2 ch at end
of previous round, *1 ch, 1 beaded ch, 1 ch, 1 dc
into next ch sp, rep from * to end, replacing
dc at end of last rep with ss to first dc.
Fasten off.

TO MAKE UP
Press very carefully following instructions on
ball band, taking care not to damage the beads.
Join shoulder seams.

Armhole Edgings (Both alike)
With RS facing and using 2.50 mm hook,
rejoin M at underarm point, 1 ch (does NOT
count as st), work one round of dc evenly
around entire armhole edge, ending with ss
to first dc, turn.
Round 1: (WS) 1 ch (does NOT count as st),
1 dc into each dc to end, ss to first dc.
Fasten off.

Neck Edging and Flounce
With RS facing and using 2.50 mm hook, rejoin
M at one shoulder seam, 1 ch (does NOT count
as st), work one round of dc evenly around entire
neck edge, ensuring there are an even number
of dc and ending with ss to first dc, turn.
Set this ball of yarn aside to complete neck
edging.
Thread teardrop beads onto B.
Join in B and work flounce as follows:-

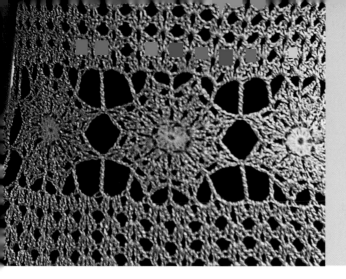

Round 1: (WS) Working into back loops only of previous round (those nearest RS of work) and using B, 3 ch (counts as first tr), (1 tr, 2 ch and 2 tr) into first dc, *miss 1 dc, (2 tr, 2 ch and 2 tr) into next dc, rep from * to last dc, miss last dc, ss to top of 3 ch at beg of round, turn.

Round 2: Using B, ss across and into first ch sp, 3 ch (counts as first tr), (1 tr, 2 ch and 2 tr) into same ch sp, *1 beaded ch**, (2 tr, 2 ch and 2 tr) into next ch sp, rep from * to end, ending last rep at **, ss to top of 3 ch at beg of round, turn. Join in second ball of M.

Round 3: Using M, 1 ch (does NOT count as st), 1 dc into last ch sp of previous round placing this dc so that it sits after bead, *3 ch, 1 dc into next 2-ch sp, 3 ch**, (1 dc, 3 ch and 1 dc) into next beaded ch sp ensuring bead sits between the 2 dc, rep from * to end, ending last rep at **, 1 dc into next beaded ch sp placing this dc before the beaded ch, 2 ch, 1 dc into first dc, turn.

Round 4: Using M, 1 ch (does NOT count as st), 1 dc into ch sp partly formed by 2 ch at end of previous round, *3 ch, 1 dc into next ch sp, rep from * until dc has been worked into last 3-ch sp, 2 ch, 1 dc into first dc, turn. Break off M.

Rounds 5 and 6: Using B, as round 4. Join in A.

Rounds 7 and 8: Using A, as round 4. Break off A.

Rounds 9 and 10: Using B, as round 4. Thread round beads onto B.

Round 11: Using B, 1 ch (does NOT count as st), 1 dc into ch sp partly formed by 2 ch at end of previous round, *1 ch, 1 beaded ch, 1 ch, 1 dc into next ch sp, rep from * to end, replacing dc at end of last rep with ss to first dc. Fasten off.

Pick up ball of M left at end of first round of Edging and Flounce and, with WS facing, complete Neck Edging as follows:- 1 ch (does NOT count as st), working into rem free loop of dc already used for Flounce and into both loops of each dc between those used for Flounce (so leaving flounce sitting on RS of work) work 1 dc into each dc to end, ss to first dc. Fasten off.

Keep your shoulders warm in this chevron stitch capelet. The soft yarn combines a glittering golden thread with the cuddliest of yarns to add just a dash of sparkle.

Capelet

★☆☆ EASY

MEASUREMENTS

One size, to fit bust
86–107 cm
34–42 in

Actual width at lower edge
149.5 cm
58³/₄ in

Actual length
44 cm
17¹/₄ in

MATERIALS

- 6 × 50 g balls of RYC Soft Lux in Basalt 005
- 5.00 mm crochet hook

TENSION

Based on a treble fabric tension of 14¹/₂ sts and 7¹/₂ rows to 10 cm (4 in) using 5.00 mm hook. Change hook size if necessary to obtain this tension.

ABBREVIATIONS

See page 15.

Neck Border and Ties

With 5.00 mm hook, make 168 ch.
Row 1: (RS) 1 dc into 2nd ch from hook, 1 dc into each ch to end, turn. 167 sts.
Row 2: 1 ch (does NOT count as st), 1 dc into each dc to end.
Fasten off.
These 2 rows complete Neck Border and Ties.

Main Section

With RS facing, miss first 44 dc of Row 2, rejoin yarn to next dc and cont as follows:-
Row 1: (RS) 3 ch (counts as first tr), 1 tr into dc at base of 3 ch, *1 tr into each of next 2 dc, miss 1 dc, 1 tr into each of next 2 dc, (1 tr, 2 ch and 1 tr) into next dc, rep from * 11 times more, 1 tr into each of next 2 dc, miss 1 dc, 1 tr into each of next 2 dc, 2 tr into next dc and turn, leaving rem 44 dc unworked. 104 sts, 13 patt reps in total.
Row 2: 3 ch (counts as first tr), 1 tr into tr at base of 3 ch, *1 tr into each of next 2 tr, miss 2 tr, 1 tr into each of next 2 tr**, (1 tr, 2 ch and 1 tr) into next ch sp, rep from * to end, ending last rep at **, 2 tr into top of 3 ch at beg of previous row, turn.
Row 3: 3 ch (counts as first tr), 2 tr into tr at base of 3 ch, *1 tr into each of next 2 tr, miss 2 tr, 1 tr into each of next 2 tr**, (2 tr, 2 ch and

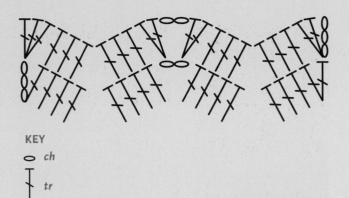

- Made from a really soft extra fine merino wool, angora and nylon mix – with just a touch of shimmering glitz – this capelet is the perfect way to keep warm but still look elegant!
- As this capelet is worked in mainly trebles and uses quite a thick yarn you'll be amazed at just how quickly it will grow.
- Worked from the neck downwards, you could easily carry on and work a few more rows if you wanted a longer length.
- Because this capelet is made all in one piece there are no seams to sew up afterwards. Just crochet it and go!

KEY

o ch

⊤ tr

2 tr) into next ch sp, rep from * to end, ending last rep at **, 3 tr into top of 3 ch at beg of previous row, turn. 130 sts.

Row 4: 3 ch (counts as first tr), 1 tr into tr at base of 3 ch, *1 tr into each of next 3 tr, miss 2 tr, 1 tr into each of next 3 tr**, (1 tr, 2 ch and 1 tr) into next ch sp, rep from * to end, ending last rep at **, 2 tr into top of 3 ch at beg of previous row, turn.

Row 5: 3 ch (counts as first tr), 2 tr into tr at base of 3 ch, *1 tr into each of next 3 tr, miss 2 tr, 1 tr into each of next 3 tr**, (2 tr, 2 ch and 2 tr) into next ch sp, rep from * to end, ending last rep at **, 3 tr into top of 3 ch at beg of previous row, turn. 156 sts.

Rows 6 and 7: 3 ch (counts as first tr), 1 tr into tr at base of 3 ch, *1 tr into each of next 4 tr, miss 2 tr, 1 tr into each of next 4 tr**, (1 tr, 2 ch and 1 tr) into next ch sp, rep from * to end, ending last rep at **, 2 tr into top of 3 ch at beg of previous row, turn.

Row 8: 3 ch (counts as first tr), 2 tr into tr at base of 3 ch, *1 tr into each of next 4 tr, miss 2 tr, 1 tr into each of next 4 tr**, (2 tr, 2 ch and 2 tr) into next ch sp, rep from * to end, ending last rep at **, 3 tr into top of 3 ch at beg of previous row, turn. 182 sts.

Rows 9 to 11: 3 ch (counts as first tr), 1 tr into tr at base of 3 ch, *1 tr into each of next 5 tr,

miss 2 tr, 1 tr into each of next 5 tr**, (1 tr, 2 ch and 1 tr) into next ch sp, rep from * to end, ending last rep at **, 2 tr into top of 3 ch at beg of previous row, turn.

Row 12: 3 ch (counts as first tr), 2 tr into tr at base of 3 ch, *1 tr into each of next 5 tr, miss 2 tr, 1 tr into each of next 5 tr**, (2 tr, 2 ch and 2 tr) into next ch sp, rep from * to end, ending last rep at **, 3 tr into top of 3 ch at beg of previous row, turn. 208 sts.

Rows 13 to 16: 3 ch (counts as first tr), 1 tr into tr at base of 3 ch, *1 tr into each of next 6 tr, miss 2 tr, 1 tr into each of next 6 tr**, (1 tr, 2 ch and 1 tr) into next ch sp, rep from * to end, ending last rep at **, 2 tr into top of 3 ch at beg of previous row, turn.

Row 17: 3 ch (counts as first tr), 2 tr into tr at base of 3 ch, *1 tr into each of next 6 tr, miss 2 tr, 1 tr into each of next 6 tr**, (2 tr, 2 ch and 2 tr) into next ch sp, rep from * to end, ending last rep at **, 3 tr into top of 3 ch at beg of previous row, turn. 234 sts.

Rows 18 to 22: 3 ch (counts as first tr), 1 tr into tr at base of 3 ch, *1 tr into each of next 7 tr, miss 2 tr, 1 tr into each of next 7 tr**, (1 tr, 2 ch and 1 tr) into next ch sp, rep from * to end, ending last rep at **, 2 tr into top of 3 ch at beg of previous row, turn.

Row 23: 3 ch (counts as first tr), 2 tr into tr at base of 3 ch, *1 tr into each of next 7 tr, miss 2 tr, 1 tr into each of next 7 tr**, (2 tr, 2 ch and 2 tr) into next ch sp, rep from * to end, ending last rep at **, 3 tr into top of 3 ch at beg of previous row, turn. 260 sts.

Rows 24 to 33: 3 ch (counts as first tr), 1 tr into tr at base of 3 ch, *1 tr into each of next 8 tr, miss 2 tr, 1 tr into each of next 8 tr**, (1 tr, 2 ch and 1 tr) into next ch sp, rep from * to end, ending last rep at **, 2 tr into top of 3 ch at beg of previous row, turn.

Turning work again so that RS of work is facing, work 1 row of crab st (dc worked from left to right, instead of right to left) along top of last row, working into each tr and ch of previous row.

Fasten off.

TO MAKE UP

Press carefully following instructions on ball band.

Made in a stunning eyelash yarn that combines classic cream with opalescent shimmer, this little shrug will ensure you look stylish but remain cosy and warm.

Shrug

MEASUREMENTS

To fit bust

81–86	91–97	102–107	cm
32–34	36–38	40–42	in

Actual size, measured from cuff to cuff

132	142	148	cm
52	56	58¹/₄	in

Actual width of section worked in rows

40	42	44	cm
15³/₄	16¹/₂	17¹/₄	in

MATERIALS

- 6 (6: 7) × 50 g balls of Wendy Chic in cream 257
- 7.00 mm crochet hook

TENSION

9 sts and 7 rows to 10 cm (4 in) measured over pattern using 7.00 mm hook. Change hook size if necessary to obtain this tension.

ABBREVIATIONS

tr2tog – *yoh and insert hook as indicated, yoh and draw loop through, yoh and draw through 2 loops, rep from * once more, yoh and draw through all 3 loops on hook.

See also page 15.

Shrug is worked in one piece from cuff to cuff

With 7.00 mm hook, make 20 (22: 22) ch and join with a ss to form a ring.

Round 1: (RS) 3 ch (counts as first tr), miss first ch, 1 tr into each ch to end, ss to top of 3 ch at beg of round, turn. 20 (22: 22) sts.

Cont in patt as follows:

Round 2: (WS) ss between 3 ch at beg and tr at end of previous round, 3 ch (counts as first tr), 1 tr between last 2 tr of previous round, *1 tr between next 2 tr, rep from * until tr has been worked between 3 ch and tr at beg of previous round, ss to top of 3 ch at beg of round, turn. This round forms patt – trs worked between trs of previous round.

Cont in patt for a further 2 rounds.

Round 5: ss between 3 ch at beg and tr at end of previous round, 3 ch (counts as first tr), 1 tr into same place as ss – 1 st increased, 1 tr between last tr of previous round and next tr, *1 tr between next 2 tr, rep from * until tr has been worked between 3 ch and tr at beg of previous round, 1 tr into same place as last tr – 1 st increased, ss to top of 3 ch at beg of round, turn. 22 (24: 24) sts.

Working all increases as set by last round, inc 1 st at each end of every 3rd round until there are 36 (38: 40) sts.

Work 4 (6: 3) rounds – 30 (32: 32) rounds completed. Work should measure 43 (46: 46) cm, 17 (18: 18) in.

Now work patt in rows, not rounds, as follows:

Next row: 3 ch (counts as first tr), 1 tr between last 2 tr of previous row, *1 tr between next 2 tr, rep from * until tr has been worked between 3 ch and tr at beg of previous row, turn.

This row forms patt worked in rows.

Work a further 30 (33: 37) rows.

Next row: 3 ch (counts as first tr), 1 tr between last 2 tr of previous row, *1 tr between next 2 tr, rep from * until tr has been worked between 3 ch and tr at beg of previous row, ss to top of 3 ch at beg of round, turn.

Work should measure 46 (50: 56) cm, 18 (19½: 22) in, along row-end edges.

Now working patt in rounds as before, not rows, cont as follows:

Work 4 (6: 3) rounds.

Next round: ss between 3 ch at beg and tr at end of previous round, 3 ch (does NOT count as st), 1 tr between last tr of previous round and next tr – 1 st decreased, *1 tr between next 2 tr, rep from * until tr has been worked

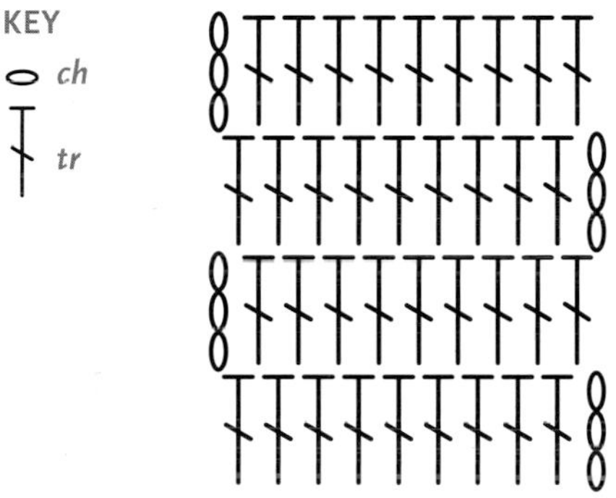

between first 2 tr of previous round, tr2tog working first "leg" between next 2 tr and 2nd "leg" between 3 ch and tr at beg of previous round – 1 st decreased, ss to top of 3 ch at beg of round, turn. 34 (36: 38) sts.

Working all decreases as set by last round, dec 1 st at each end of every 3rd round until 20 (22: 22) sts rem.

Work a further 4 rounds.

Fasten off.

TO MAKE UP

Do NOT press.

KEY

○ ch

┬ tr

This simple belt is made up of a row of bead encrusted flower motifs, worked in a casual cotton yarn. Vary the length by adding more or working fewer motifs to make the size that fits you.

Flower Motif Belt

MEASUREMENTS

Actual size
7 × 156 cm
$2^3/_4$ × $61^1/_2$ in

MATERIALS

- 1 × 50 g ball of Rowan Cotton Glace in each of colour A (magenta 818), colour B (purple 815), and colour C (black 727)
- Faceted beads: 96 in each of 2 colours for Star Motifs, and 88 in 3rd colour for Joining Motifs
- 2.50 mm crochet hook

TENSION

Star Motif measures 7 cm ($2^3/_4$ in) in diameter (excluding beads) on 2.50 mm hook. Change hook size if necessary to obtain this tension.

ABBREVIATIONS

See page 15.

For how to work with beads, see pages 16–17.

STAR MOTIF

Thread 16 beads onto yarn A – 8 of one colour for outer edge and 8 of second colour for centre. With 2.50 mm hook and yarn A, make 4 ch and join with a ss to form a ring.

Round 1: (RS) 1 ch (does NOT count as st), [1 dc into ring, 1 beaded ch – make sure bead is left sitting on RS of work] 8 times, ss to first dc.
Round 2: 7 ch (counts as first tr and 4 ch), miss dc at base of 7 ch and next beaded ch, *1 tr into next dc, 4 ch, miss 1 beaded ch, rep from * to end, ss to 3rd of 7 ch at beg of round. 8 ch sps.
Round 3: 1 ch (does NOT count as st), (1 dc, 1 htr, 1 tr, 1 dtr, 1 beaded ch, 1 dtr, 1 tr, 1 htr and 1 dc) into each ch sp to end, ss to first dc.
Fasten off.
Motif is an 8-pointed star shape with a bead sitting at the end of each point.
Make a further 11 motifs in this way, making another 5 using yarn A and 6 using yarn B.

JOINING MOTIF

Star Motifs are joined to these Motifs as round 3 is worked.
Thread 8 beads onto yarn C.
With 2.50 mm hook and yarn C, make 6 ch and join with a ss to form a ring.
Round 1: (RS) 1 ch (does NOT count as st), 16 dc into ring, ss to first dc.
Round 2: 1 ch (does NOT count as st), 1 dc into dc at base of 1 ch, 1 dc into next dc, *(1 dc, 8 ch and 1 dc) into next dc**, 1 dc into each of next 3 dc, rep from * to end, ending last rep at **, 1 dc into next dc, ss to first dc.

Round 3: 1 ch (does NOT count as st), 1 dc into dc at base of 1 ch, *miss 2 dc, (2 htr, 3 tr, 1 beaded ch, 5 tr, 1 beaded ch and 5 tr) into next ch sp, 1 ss into beaded ch at end of one point of a Star Motif worked in yarn A, (3 tr and 2 htr) into same ch sp, miss 2 dc, 1 dc into next dc, miss 2 dc, (2 htr and 3 tr) into next ch sp, 1 ss into beaded ch at end of next point of same Star Motif worked in yarn A, (5 tr, 1 beaded ch, 5 tr, 1 beaded ch, 3 tr and 2 htr) into same ch sp, miss 2 dc, 1 dc into next dc, miss 2 dc, (2 htr, 3 tr, 1 beaded ch, 5 tr, 1 beaded ch and 5 tr) into next ch sp, 1 ss into beaded ch at end of one point of a Star Motif worked in yarn B, (3 tr and 2 htr) into same ch sp, miss 2 dc, 1 dc into next dc, miss 2 dc, (2 htr and 3 tr) into next ch sp, 1 ss into beaded ch at end of next point of same Star Motif worked in yarn B, (5 tr, 1 beaded ch, 5 tr, 1 beaded ch, 3 tr and 2 htr) into same ch sp, miss 2 dc, ss to first dc. Fasten off.

Make a further 10 Joining Motifs in this way, joining them to form one long strip of 23 alternating Star and Joining Motifs, using alternating colours of Star Motifs and ensuring there are 2 points of each Star Motif left free between those joined to Joining Motifs.

TO MAKE UP
Press following instructions on ball band.

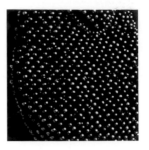

Totally covered in iridescent beads, this pouch bag is made all in one piece so there's no sewing up afterwards! It's worked in rounds of beaded chain and double crochet using a fine lurex yarn.

Beaded Evening Bag

★★★ ADVANCED

MEASUREMENTS

Actual size, excluding tassel
17 × 19 cm
6³/₄ × 7¹/₂ in

MATERIALS

- 3 × 25 g balls of Rowan Lurex Shimmer in Black 334
- 2.50 mm crochet hook
- Approx 2,900 beads

TENSION

24 sts and 27 rows to 10 cm (4 in) measured over beaded pattern using 2.50 mm hook. Change hook size if necessary to obtain this tension.

ABBREVIATIONS

dc2tog - *insert hook as indicated, yoh and draw loop through, rep from * once more, yoh and draw through all 3 loops on hook. See also page 15. For how to work with beads, see pages 16–17.*

MAIN SECTION

With 2.50 mm hook, make 8 ch, ss in first ch to form a ring.
Foundation round: (WS) 1 ch (does NOT count as st), 2 dc into each ch to end, ss to first dc, turn. 16 sts.

Cont in beaded patt as follows:
Round 1: (RS) 1 ch (does NOT count as st), 1 dc into each of first 2 dc, [1 beaded ch, 1 dc into each of next 2 dc] 3 times, [1 dc into each of next 2 dc, 1 beaded ch] 3 times, 1 dc into each of last 2 dc, ss to first dc, turn. (NOTE: Whilst working the patt, the beaded ch do NOT count as sts. When working across top of foll rounds, miss the beaded ch and only work into the dc of previous rounds. Ensure all beads sit on RS of work by gently easing them through to that side of the work.)
Round 2: 1 ch (does NOT count as st), 2 dc into first dc, [1 beaded ch, 1 dc into each of next 2 dc] 3 times, 1 beaded ch, 2 dc into each of next 2 dc, [1 beaded ch, 1 dc into each of next 2 dc] 3 times, 1 beaded ch, 2 dc into last dc, ss to first dc, turn. 20 sts.
Round 3: 1 ch (does NOT count as st), 2 dc into first dc, [1 beaded ch, 1 dc into each of next 2 dc] 4 times, 1 beaded ch, 2 dc into each of next 2 dc, [1 beaded ch, 1 dc into each of next 2 dc] 4 times, 1 beaded ch, 2 dc into last dc, ss to first dc, turn. 24 sts.
Round 4: 1 ch (does NOT count as st), 2 dc into first dc, [1 beaded ch, 1 dc into each of next 2 dc] 5 times, 1 beaded ch, 2 dc into each of next 2 dc, [1 beaded ch, 1 dc into each of next 2 dc] 5 times, 1 beaded ch, 2 dc into last dc, ss to first dc, turn. 28 sts.

Round 5: 1 ch (does NOT count as st), 2 dc into first dc, [1 beaded ch, 1 dc into each of next 2 dc] 6 times, 1 beaded ch, 2 dc into each of next 2 dc, [1 beaded ch, 1 dc into each of next 2 dc] 6 times, 1 beaded ch, 2 dc into last dc, ss to first dc, turn. 32 sts.

Cont in this way, increasing 4 sts on every round, until the foll round has been worked:

Round 13: 1 ch (does NOT count as st), 2 dc into first dc, [1 beaded ch, 1 dc into each of next 2 dc] 14 times, 1 beaded ch, 2 dc into each of next 2 dc, [1 beaded ch, 1 dc into each of next 2 dc] 14 times, 1 beaded ch, 2 dc into last dc, ss to first dc, turn. 64 sts.

Round 14: 1 ch (does NOT count as st), 1 dc into first dc, [1 beaded ch, 1 dc into each of next 2 dc] 31 times, 1 beaded ch, 1 dc into last dc, ss to first dc, turn.

Round 15: 1 ch (does NOT count as st), 2 dc into first dc, 1 dc into next dc, [1 beaded ch, 1 dc into each of next 2 dc] 14 times, 1 beaded ch, 1 dc into next dc, 2 dc into each of next 2 dc, 1 dc into next dc, [1 beaded ch, 1 dc into each of next 2 dc] 14 times, 1 beaded ch, 1 dc into next dc, 2 dc into last dc, ss to first dc, turn. 68 sts.

Round 16: 1 ch (does NOT count as st), 1 dc into each of first 2 dc, [1 beaded ch, 1 dc into each of next 2 dc] 16 times, 1 dc into each of next 2 dc, [1 beaded ch, 1 dc into each of next 2 dc] 16 times, ss to first dc, turn.

Round 17: 1 ch (does NOT count as st), 2 dc into first dc, [1 beaded ch, 1 dc into each of next 2 dc] 16 times, 1 beaded ch, 2 dc into each of next 2 dc, [1 beaded ch, 1 dc into each of next 2 dc] 16 times, 1 beaded ch, 2 dc into last dc, ss to first dc, turn. 72 sts.

Round 18: 1 ch (does NOT count as st), 1 dc into first dc, [1 beaded ch, 1 dc into each of next 2 dc] 35 times, 1 beaded ch, 1 dc into last dc, ss to first dc, turn.

Round 19: 1 ch (does NOT count as st), 2 dc into first dc, 1 dc into next dc, [1 beaded ch, 1 dc into each of next 2 dc] 16 times, 1 beaded ch, 1 dc into next dc, 2 dc into each of next 2 dc, 1 dc into next dc, [1 beaded ch, 1 dc into each of next 2 dc] 16 times, 1 beaded ch, 1 dc into next dc, 2 dc into last dc, ss to first dc, turn. 76 sts.

Round 20: 1 ch (does NOT count as st), 1 dc into each of first 2 dc, [1 beaded ch, 1 dc into each of next 2 dc] 18 times, 1 dc into each of next 2 dc, [1 beaded ch, 1 dc into each of next 2 dc] 18 times, ss to first dc, turn.

Round 21: 1 ch (does NOT count as st), 1 dc into first dc, [1 beaded ch, 1 dc into each of next 2 dc] 37 times, 1 beaded ch, 1 dc into last dc, ss to first dc, turn.

Round 22: As round 20.

Round 23: 1 ch (does NOT count as st), 2 dc into first dc, [1 beaded ch, 1 dc into each of next 2 dc] 18 times, 1 beaded ch, 2 dc into each of next 2 dc, [1 beaded ch, 1 dc into each of next 2 dc] 18 times, 1 beaded ch, 2 dc into last dc, ss to first dc, turn. 80 sts.

Round 24: 1 ch (does NOT count as st), 1 dc

+◎+   +◎+   +◎+   +◎+   +◎+   +◎+
+   +◎+   +◎+   +◎+   +◎+   +◎+   +
+◎+   +◎+   +◎+   +◎+   +◎+   +◎+
+   +◎+   +◎+   +◎+   +◎+   +◎+   +
+◎+   +◎+   +◎+   +◎+   +◎+   +◎+

into first dc, [1 beaded ch, 1 dc into each of next 2 dc] 39 times, 1 beaded ch, 1 dc into last dc, ss to first dc, turn.

Round 25: 1 ch (does NOT count as st), 1 dc into each of first 2 dc, [1 beaded ch, 1 dc into each of next 2 dc] 19 times, 1 dc into each of next 2 dc, [1 beaded ch, 1 dc into each of next 2 dc] 19 times, ss to first dc, turn.

Rounds 26 to 29: As rounds 24 and 25, twice.

Round 30: As round 24.

Round 31: 1 ch (does NOT count as st), dc2tog over first 2 dc, [1 beaded ch, 1 dc into each of next 2 dc] 18 times, 1 beaded ch, [dc2tog over next 2 dc] twice, [1 beaded ch, 1 dc into each of next 2 dc] 18 times, 1 beaded ch, dc2tog over last 2 dc, ss to first dc2tog, turn. 76 sts.

Rounds 32 and 33: As rounds 20 and 21.

Round 34: As round 20.

Round 35: 1 ch (does NOT count as st), dc2tog over first 2 dc, 1 dc into next dc, [1 beaded ch, 1 dc into each of next 2 dc] 16 times, 1 beaded ch, 1 dc into next dc, [dc2tog over next 2 dc] twice, 1 dc into next dc, [1 beaded ch, 1 dc into each of next 2 dc] 16 times, 1 beaded ch, 1 dc into next dc, dc2tog over last 2 dc, ss to first dc2tog, turn. 72 sts.

Round 36: As round 18.

Round 37: 1 ch (does NOT count as st), 1 dc into each of first 2 dc, [1 beaded ch, 1 dc into each of next 2 dc] 17 times, 1 dc into each of next 2 dc, [1 beaded ch, 1 dc into each of next 2 dc] 17 times, ss to first dc, turn.

Round 38: As round 18.

Round 39: 1 ch (does NOT count as st), dc2tog over first 2 dc, [1 beaded ch, 1 dc into each of next 2 dc] 16 times, 1 beaded ch, [dc2tog over next 2 dc] twice, [1 beaded ch, 1 dc into each of next 2 dc] 16 times, 1 beaded ch, dc2tog over last 2 dc, ss to first dc, turn. 68 sts.

Round 40: As round 16.

Round 41: 1 ch (does NOT count as st), 1 dc into first dc, [1 beaded ch, 1 dc into each of next 2 dc] 33 times, 1 beaded ch, 1 dc into last dc, ss to first dc, turn.

Round 42: As round 16.

Round 43: 1 ch (does NOT count as st), dc2tog over first 2 dc, 1 dc into next dc, [1 beaded ch, 1 dc into each of next 2 dc] 14 times, 1 beaded ch, 1 dc into next dc, [dc2tog over next 2 dc] twice, 1 dc into next dc, [1 beaded ch, 1 dc into each of next 2 dc] 14 times, 1 beaded ch, 1 dc into next dc, dc2tog over last 2 dc, ss to first dc2tog, turn. 64 sts.

Round 44: As round 14.

Round 45: 1 ch (does NOT count as st), 1 dc into each of first 2 dc, [1 beaded ch, 1 dc into each of next 2 dc] 15 times, 1 dc into each of next 2 dc, [1 beaded ch, 1 dc into each of next 2 dc] 15 times, ss to first dc, turn.

Round 46: As round 14.

Round 47: 1 ch (does NOT count as st), dc2tog over first 2 dc, [1 beaded ch, 1 dc into each of next 2 dc] 14 times, 1 beaded ch, [dc2tog over next 2 dc] twice, [1 beaded ch, 1 dc into each of next 2 dc] 14 times, 1 beaded ch, dc2tog over last 2 dc, ss to first dc2tog, turn. 60 sts.

■ This bag uses beads with an oil-on-water finish to them but you could make a brighter, funky version by using a selection of different coloured beads. Mix them all together before you start threading them onto the yarn and thread them so that the colours appear randomly.
■ The bag is quite heavy as there are so many beads – so make sure you attach the strap securely!

Round 48: 1 ch (does NOT count as st), 1 dc into each of first 2 dc, [1 beaded ch, 1 dc into each of next 2 dc] 14 times, 1 dc into each of next 2 dc, [1 beaded ch, 1 dc into each of next 2 dc] 14 times, ss to first dc, turn.

Round 49: 1 ch (does NOT count as st), 1 dc into first dc, [1 beaded ch, 1 dc into each of next 2 dc] 29 times, 1 beaded ch, 1 dc into last dc, ss to first dc, turn.

Round 50: As round 48.

Shape flap

Row 51: (RS) 1 ch (does NOT count as st), 1 dc into first dc, [1 beaded ch, 1 dc into each of next 2 dc] 14 times, 1 beaded ch, 1 dc into next dc, **turn**.

Work in rows on this set of 30 sts only for flap.

Row 52: 1 ch (does NOT count as st), 1 dc into each of first 2 dc, [1 beaded ch, 1 dc into each of next 2 dc] 14 times, turn.

Row 53: 1 ch (does NOT count as st), 1 dc into first dc, [1 beaded ch, 1 dc into each of next 2 dc] 14 times, 1 beaded ch, 1 dc into last dc, turn.

Rows 54 and 55: As rows 52 and 53.

Row 56: As row 52.

Row 57: 1 ch (does NOT count as st), dc2tog over first 2 dc, 1 dc into next dc, [1 beaded ch, 1 dc into each of next 2 dc] 12 times, 1 beaded ch, 1 dc into next dc, dc2tog over last 2 dc, turn. 28 sts.

Row 58: 1 ch (does NOT count as st), 1 dc into first dc, [1 beaded ch, 1 dc into each of next 2 dc] 13 times, 1 beaded ch, 1 dc into last dc, turn.

Row 59: 1 ch (does NOT count as st), dc2tog over first 2 dc, [1 beaded ch, 1 dc into each of next 2 dc] 12 times, 1 beaded ch, dc2tog over last 2 dc, turn. 26 sts.

Row 60: 1 ch (does NOT count as st), 1 dc into each of first 2 dc, [1 beaded ch, 1 dc into each of next 2 dc] 12 times, turn.

Row 61: 1 ch (does NOT count as st), dc2tog over first 2 dc, 1 dc into next dc, [1 beaded ch, 1 dc into each of next 2 dc] 10 times, 1 beaded ch, 1 dc into next dc, dc2tog over last 2 dc, turn. 24 sts.

Row 62: 1 ch (does NOT count as st), 1 dc into first dc, [1 beaded ch, 1 dc into each of next 2 dc] 11 times, 1 beaded ch, 1 dc into last dc, turn.

Row 63: 1 ch (does NOT count as st), dc2tog over first 2 dc, [1 beaded ch, 1 dc into each of next 2 dc] 10 times, 1 beaded ch, dc2tog over last 2 dc, turn. 22 sts.

Row 64: 1 ch (does NOT count as st), dc2tog over first 2 dc, [1 beaded ch, 1 dc into each of next 2 dc] 9 times, 1 beaded ch, dc2tog over last 2 dc, turn. 20 sts.

Row 65: 1 ch (does NOT count as st), dc2tog over first 2 dc, [1 beaded ch, 1 dc into each of next 2 dc] 8 times, 1 beaded ch, dc2tog over last 2 dc, turn. 18 sts.

Row 66: 1 ch (does NOT count as st), dc2tog over first 2 dc, [1 beaded ch, 1 dc into each of next 2 dc] 7 times, 1 beaded ch, dc2tog over last 2 dc, turn. 16 sts.

Row 67: 1 ch (does NOT count as st), dc2tog over first 2 dc, [1 beaded ch, 1 dc into each of

next 2 dc] 6 times, 1 beaded ch, dc2tog over last 2 dc, turn. 14 sts.

Row 68: 1 ch (does NOT count as st), dc2tog over first 2 dc, [1 beaded ch, 1 dc into each of next 2 dc] 5 times, 1 beaded ch, dc2tog over last 2 dc, turn. 12 sts.

Row 69: 1 ch (does NOT count as st), dc2tog over first 2 dc, [1 beaded ch, 1 dc into each of next 2 dc] 4 times, 1 beaded ch, dc2tog over last 2 dc, turn. 10 sts.

Row 70: 1 ch (does NOT count as st), dc2tog over first 2 dc, [1 beaded ch, 1 dc into each of next 2 dc] 3 times, 1 beaded ch, dc2tog over last 2 dc, turn. 8 sts.

Row 71: 1 ch (does NOT count as st), dc2tog over first 2 dc, [1 beaded ch, 1 dc into each of next 2 dc] twice, 1 beaded ch, dc2tog over last 2 dc, turn. 6 sts.

Row 72: 1 ch (does NOT count as st), dc2tog over first 2 dc, 1 beaded ch, 1 dc into each of next 2 dc, 1 beaded ch, dc2tog over last 2 dc, turn. 4 sts.

Row 73: 1 ch (does NOT count as st), dc2tog over first 2 dc, dc2tog over last 2 dc. 2 sts. Fasten off.

FLAP AND OPENING EDGING

With 2.50 mm hook and RS facing, attach yarn to Main Section on first dc after turning point for flap, 1 ch (does NOT count as st), 1 dc into dc where yarn was rejoined, 1 dc into each of next 29 dc of round 50, then work in dc evenly around outer shaped edge of flap,

ending with ss to first dc, turn.

Next round: (WS) 1 ch (does NOT count as st), 1 beaded dc into each dc to end, ss to first dc. Fasten off.

BASE TASSEL

With 2.50 mm hook and **WS** facing, attach yarn to foundation ch edge of Main Section, 1 ch (does NOT count as st), 1 beaded dc into each of 8 foundation ch, ss to first dc, do NOT turn.

Next round: (WS) 1 ch (does NOT count as st), 1 beaded dc into each beaded dc to end, ss to first dc, do NOT turn.

Rep last round twice more.

Work fringe

Next round: Slide 40–50 beads up next to ss closing last round and work a ss into first st of last round leaving beads to form a loop, *slide another 40–50 beads by next to last ss and work a ss into next st leaving beads to form a loop, rep from * 6 times more. Fasten off.

STRAP

With 2.50 mm hook, make 201 ch.

Row 1: (RS) 1 beaded dc into 2nd ch from hook, 1 beaded dc into each ch to end, turn.

Row 2: 1 ch (does NOT count as st), 1 dc into first beaded dc, 1 dc into each beaded dc to end, turn.

Row 3: 1 ch (does NOT count as st), 1 beaded dc into each dc to end. Fasten off.

Attach ends of Strap inside upper edge of Main Section as in photograph.

Combine toning shades of pink and purple lurex yarns with twinkling beads to make this stunning flower. Complete with leaves and twirling tendrils it's sure to jazz up any outfit.

CORSAGE

MEASUREMENTS

Actual size, excluding streamers
14 × 19 cm
5^1/$_2$ × 7^1/$_2$ in

MATERIALS

- 1 × 50 g ball of Twilleys Goldfingering in each of pink 62, lilac 56, purple 60 and green 51
- 2.50 mm crochet hook
- Approx 210 clear, 50 pink, 230 green, and 80 purple beads
- Brooch back

TENSION

Flower Centre measures 5 cm (2 in) in diameter using 2.50 mm hook. Change hook size if necessary to obtain this tension.

ABBREVIATIONS

dc2tog=*insert hook as indicated, yoh and draw loop through, rep from * once more, yoh and draw through all 3 loops on hook; dc3tog=*insert hook as indicated, yoh and draw loop through, rep from *twice more, yoh and draw through all 4 loops on hook. *See also page 15.*

For how to work with beads, see pages 16–17.

FLOWER CENTRE

Thread 96 assorted pink and clear beads onto pink yarn.
With 2.50 mm hook and pink, make 4 ch and join with a ss to form a ring.
Round 1: (RS) 1 ch (does NOT count as st), 8 dc into ring, ss to first dc. 8 sts.
Round 2: 1 ch (does NOT count as st), 3 dc into each dc to end, ss to first dc. 24 sts.
Round 3: 3 ch (counts as first tr), 3 tr into dc at base of 3 ch, 4 tr into each dc to end, ss to top of 3 ch at beg of round. 96 sts.
Round 4: 1 ch (does NOT count as st), 1 dc into first st, *1 ch, 1 beaded ch, 1 ch, 1 dc into next tr, rep from * to end, replacing dc at end of last rep with ss to first dc.
Fasten off.

SMALL PETALS

Thread 85 clear beads onto lilac yarn.
With 2.50 mm hook and lilac, make 4 ch and join with a ss to form a ring.
Round 1: (RS) 1 ch (does NOT count as st), 10 dc into ring, ss to first dc. 10 sts.
Round 2: 6 ch (counts as first tr and 3 ch), miss dc at base of 6 ch and next dc, [1 tr into next dc, 3 ch, miss 1 dc] 4 times, ss to 3rd of 6 ch at beg of round. 5 ch sps.

Work petals

Row 1: (RS) ss into first ch sp, 1 ch (does NOT count as st), 5 dc into same ch sp, turn.

Row 2: 1 ch (does NOT count as st), 2 dc into each of first 2 dc, 1 dc into next dc, 2 dc into each of last 2 dc, turn. 9 sts.

Row 3: 1 ch (does NOT count as st), 2 dc into first dc, 1 dc into each of next 7 dc, 2 dc into last dc, turn. 11 sts.

Row 4: 1 ch (does NOT count as st), 2 dc into first dc, 1 dc into next dc, 1 beaded dc into next dc, 1 dc into each of next 7 dc, 2 dc into last dc, turn. 13 sts.

Row 5: 1 ch (does NOT count as st), 2 dc into first dc, 1 dc into each of next 11 dc, 2 dc into last dc, turn. 15 sts.

Row 6: 1 ch (does NOT count as st), 2 dc into first dc, 1 dc into each of next 9 dc, 1 beaded dc into next dc, 1 dc into each of next 3 dc, 2 dc into last dc, turn. 17 sts.

Row 7: 1 ch (does NOT count as st), 1 dc into each dc to end, turn.

Row 8: 1 ch (does NOT count as st), 1 dc into each of first 3 dc, 1 beaded dc into next dc, 1 dc into each of next 2 dc, 1 beaded dc into next dc, 1 dc into each of last 10 dc, turn.

Row 9: As row 7.

Row 10: 1 ch (does NOT count as st), 1 dc into first dc, dc2tog over next 2 dc, 1 dc into each of next 7 dc, 1 beaded dc into next dc, 1 dc into each of next 3 dc, dc2tog over next 2 dc, 1 dc into last dc, turn. 15 sts.

Row 11: 1 ch (does NOT count as st), 1 dc into first dc, [dc2tog over next 2 sts] twice, 1 dc into each of next 5 dc, [dc2tog over next 2 sts] twice, 1 dc into last dc, turn. 11 sts.

Row 12: 1 ch (does NOT count as st), 1 dc into first dc, [dc2tog over next 2 sts] twice, 1 beaded dc into next dc, [dc2tog over next 2 sts] twice, 1 dc into last dc, turn. 7 sts.

Row 13: 1 ch (does NOT count as st), 1 dc into first dc, dc2tog over next 2 sts, 1 dc into next dc, dc2tog over next 2 sts, 1 dc into last dc, turn. 5 sts.

Row 14: 1 ch (does NOT count as st), 1 dc into first dc, dc3tog over next 3 sts, 1 dc into last dc, turn. 3 sts.

Row 15: 1 ch (does NOT count as st), dc3tog over all 3 sts and fasten off.

These 15 rows complete one petal.

*With RS facing, rejoin yarn with a ss into next ch sp of round 2, 1 ch (does NOT count as st), 5 dc into this ch sp, turn.

Now work rows 2 to 15 again.

Rep from * until 5 petals have been completed.

Work edging

With WS facing, rejoin yarn with a ss into a tr of round 2 between petals, 1 ch (does NOT count as st), work one round of dc evenly around outer edges of all petals, working into each tr of round 2 between petals, placing a bead on every 3rd dc and ending with ss to first dc. Fasten off.

Lay Flower Centre onto centre of Small Petals and sew in place as in photograph.

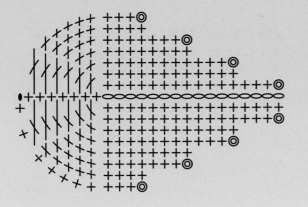

KEY
+ dc
o ch
• ss
◎ beaded ch

Leaf pattern

LARGE PETALS

Thread 150 assorted purple and clear beads onto purple yarn.

With 2.50 mm hook and purple, make 4 ch and join with a ss to form a ring.

Round 1: (RS) 1 ch (does NOT count as st), 9 dc into ring, ss to first dc. 9 sts.

Round 2: 3 ch (counts as first tr), 1 tr into base of 3 ch, 2 tr into each dc to end, ss to top of 3 ch at beg of round. 18 sts.

Round 3: 6 ch (counts as first tr and 3 ch), miss st at base of 6 ch and next tr, [1 tr into next tr, 3 ch, miss 1 tr] 8 times, ss to 3rd of 6 ch at beg of round. 9 ch sps.

Now complete as given for Small Petals from start of working petals – there will be a total of 9 petals.

Lay Flower Centre and Small Petals onto centre of Large Petals and sew in place as in photograph.

STREAMERS

Thread 200 green beads onto green yarn.

With 2.50 mm hook and green, make 31 ch, 1 beaded dc into 2nd ch from hook, 1 beaded dc into each of next 29 ch, 51 ch, 1 beaded dc into 2nd ch from hook, 1 beaded dc into each of next 49 ch, 41 ch, 1 beaded dc into 2nd ch from hook, 1 beaded dc into each of next 39 ch, 46 ch, 1 beaded dc into 2nd ch from hook, 1 beaded dc into each of next 44 ch, 36 ch, 1 beaded dc into 2nd ch from hook, 1 beaded dc into each of next 34 ch.

Fasten off.

Sew Streamers in place to back of Large Petals as in photograph.

LEAVES (Make 3)

Thread 8 green beads onto green yarn.

With 2.50 mm hook and green, make 16 ch.

Row 1: (RS) 1 beaded ch, 1 dc into 3rd ch from hook, 1 dc into each of next 13 ch, 3 dc into last ch, now working back along other side of foundation ch, 1 dc into each of next 15 ch, turn.

Row 2: 1 beaded ch, miss first dc, 1 dc into each dc to last 3 dc, working 3 dc into central dc at base of Leaf, turn.

Rows 3 to 7: As row 2.

Row 8: 1 beaded ch, miss first dc, 1 dc into each dc to central dc at base of Leaf, 1 ss into same dc as last dc.

Fasten off.

Sew Leaves to back of Large Petals as in photograph. Attach brooch back.

Completely encrusted with pearl teardrop beads, this bag will shimmer all night long! It's made in simple rounds of plain and beaded double crochet so there's very little sewing up to do afterwards.

Pearl Evening Bag

 ADVANCED

MEASUREMENTS

Actual size, approx
32.5 × 20 cm
12³/₄ × 7³/₄ in

MATERIALS

- 4 × 50 g balls of Twilleys Goldfingering in white 10
- 2.50 mm crochet hook
- Approx 2,500 pearl teardrop beads
- Piece of firm card 30 cm × 15 cm
- Piece of lining fabric 30 cm x 30 cm
- 40 cm of 3 cm wide firm petersham ribbon
- One large press stud fastener

TENSION

28 sts and 32 rows to 10 cm (4 in) measured over beaded double crochet fabric using 2.50 mm hook. Change hook size if necessary to obtain this tension.

ABBREVIATIONS

dc2tog - *insert hook as indicated, yoh and draw loop through, rep from * once more, yoh and draw through all 3 loops on hook.
See also page 15.

For how to work with beads, see pages 16–17.

MAIN SECTION

With 2.50 mm hook, make 42 ch.
Round 1: (RS) 2 dc into 2nd ch from hook, 1 dc into each of next 39 ch, 4 dc into last ch, working back along other side of foundation ch work 1 dc into each of next 39 ch, 2 dc into last ch – this is same ch as used for 2 dc at beg of round, ss to first dc, turn. 86 sts.
Round 2: 1 ch (does NOT count as st), 2 dc into each of first 2 dc, 1 dc into each of next 39 dc, 2 dc into each of next 4 dc, 1 dc into each of next 39 dc, 2 dc into each of last 2 dc, ss to first dc, turn. 94 sts.
Round 3: 1 ch (does NOT count as st), 1 dc into each dc to end, ss to first dc, turn.
Round 4: 1 ch (does NOT count as st), *[1 dc into next dc, 2 dc into next dc] twice, 1 dc into each of next 39 dc, [1 dc into next dc, 2 dc into next dc] twice, rep from * once more, ss to first dc, turn. 102 sts.
Round 5: 1 ch (does NOT count as st), *[1 dc into each of next 2 dc, 2 dc into next dc] twice, 1 dc into each of next 39 dc, [1 dc into each of next 2 dc, 2 dc into next dc] twice, rep from * once more, ss to first dc, turn. 110 sts.
Round 6: As round 3.
Round 7: 1 ch (does NOT count as st), *[1 dc into each of next 3 dc, 2 dc into next dc] twice, 1 dc into each of next 39 dc, [1 dc into each of

■ *The pearl beads are only placed on wrong side rounds so, to avoid sliding them along the yarn, try working from two balls of yarn at the same time. Thread the beads onto one ball and use this for the beaded rounds, using a plain ball for the other rounds.*

next 3 dc, 2 dc into next dc] twice, rep from * once more, ss to first dc, turn. 118 sts.

Round 8: 1 ch (does NOT count as st), *[1 dc into each of next 4 dc, 2 dc into next dc] twice, 1 dc into each of next 39 dc, [1 dc into each of next 4 dc, 2 dc into next dc] twice, rep from * once more, ss to first dc, turn. 126 sts.

Round 9: As round 3.

Round 10: 1 ch (does NOT count as st), *[1 dc into each of next 5 dc, 2 dc into next dc] twice, 1 dc into each of next 39 dc, [1 dc into each of next 5 dc, 2 dc into next dc] twice, rep from * once more, ss to first dc, turn. 134 sts.

Round 11: 1 ch (does NOT count as st), *[1 dc into each of next 6 dc, 2 dc into next dc] twice, 1 dc into each of next 39 dc, [1 dc into each of next 6 dc, 2 dc into next dc] twice, rep from * once more, ss to first dc, turn. 142 sts.

Round 12: As round 3.

Round 13: 1 ch (does NOT count as st), *[1 dc into each of next 7 dc, 2 dc into next dc] twice, 1 dc into each of next 39 dc, [1 dc into each of next 7 dc, 2 dc into next dc] twice, rep from * once more, ss to first dc, turn. 150 sts.

Round 14: 1 ch (does NOT count as st), *[1 dc into each of next 8 dc, 2 dc into next dc] twice, 1 dc into each of next 39 dc, [1 dc into each of next 8 dc, 2 dc into next dc] twice, rep from * once more, ss to first dc, turn. 158 sts.

Round 15: As round 3.

Round 16: 1 ch (does NOT count as st), *[1 dc into each of next 9 dc, 2 dc into next dc] twice, 1 dc into each of next 39 dc, [1 dc into each of next 9 dc, 2 dc into next dc] twice, rep from *

once more, ss to first dc, turn. 166 sts.

Round 17: 1 ch (does NOT count as st), *[1 dc into each of next 10 dc, 2 dc into next dc] twice, 1 dc into each of next 39 dc, [1 dc into each of next 10 dc, 2 dc into next dc] twice, rep from * once more, ss to first dc, turn. 174 sts.

Round 18: As round 3.

Round 19: 1 ch (does NOT count as st), *[1 dc into each of next 5 dc, 2 dc into next dc, 1 dc into each of next 6 dc] twice, 1 dc into each of next 39 dc, [1 dc into each of next 5 dc, 2 dc into next dc, 1 dc into each of next 6 dc] twice, rep from * once more, ss to first dc, turn. 182 sts.

Round 20: As round 3.

These 20 rounds complete base. Trace around shape of base and cut out this shape from firm card.

Round 21: 1 ch (does NOT count as st), working into back loops only of sts of previous row, 1 dc into each dc to end, ss to first dc, turn.

Cont in beaded dc fabric as follows:

Round 1: (WS) 1 ch (does NOT count as st), *1 dc into next dc, 1 beaded dc into next dc, rep from * to end, ss to first dc, turn.

Round 2: 1 ch (does NOT count as st), 1 dc into each dc to end, ss to first dc, turn.

Round 3: 1 ch (does NOT count as st), *1 beaded dc into next dc, 1 dc into next dc, rep from * to end, ss to first dc, turn.

Round 4: As round 2.

These 4 rounds form beaded dc fabric.
Work in beaded dc fabric for a further 50 rounds, ending with a RS row.

■ *If you want to totally line this bag, measure the size of the main section between the end of the base and before the top band is worked and make a note of this measurement. Adding seam allowance, cut and join a tube of lining fabric this size and sew it to the fabric base. Once the crochet section is complete, slip the lining inside the bag and run a gathering thread around the upper edge of the lining and pull it up to fit, enclosing this gathered edge under the top band before stitching it in place.*

KEY
+ dc
⊕ beaded dc

Shape top band

Next round: (WS) 1 ch (does NOT count as st), *1 dc into next dc, [dc2tog over next 2 dc] 3 times, rep from * to end, ss to first dc, turn. 104 sts.

Next round: 1 ch (does NOT count as st), 1 dc into each dc to end, ss to first dc, turn.

Rep last round 17 times more.

Fasten off.

HANDLE

With 2.50 mm hook, make 14 ch and join with a ss to form a ring.

Round 1: (RS) 1 ch (does NOT count as st), 1 dc into each dc to end. 14 sts.

Round 2: 1 dc into each dc to end.

Rep round 2 until Handle is 54 cm (21¼ in) long.

Fasten off.

TO MAKE UP

Do NOT press.

Join ends of petersham ribbon, overlapping them by 2 cm. Fold last 9 rounds of top band to inside and stitch in place, slipping loop of petersham ribbon underneath. Attach ends of Handle inside top band as in photograph. Cover card base shape with lining fabric, then insert base into bag and slip stitch in place. Attach stud fastener to close upper edge.

This simple slip of a dress, worked in a combination of trebles and a lacy mesh stitch, uses a silky yarn and has silver teardrop beads around the hem to add extra interest.

Slip Dress

INTERMEDIATE ★★☆

MEASUREMENTS

To fit bust

81	86	91	97	102	107	cm
32	34	36	38	40	42	in

Actual size, at underarm

81	86	91	96	101	106	cm
32	33³/4	35³/4	37³/4	39³/4	41³/4	in

Actual length, from shoulder (approx)

94	95	96	97	98	99	cm
37	37¹/2	37³/4	38	38¹/2	39	in

MATERIALS

- 9 (10: 11: 12: 13: 14) × 50 g balls of Twilleys Silky in black 79
- 2.00 mm crochet hook
- 310 (334: 350: 374: 390: 414) × silver teardrop pearl beads

TENSION

32 sts and 15 rows to 10 cm (4 in) measured over treble fabric using 2.00 mm hook. 4 pattern repeats to 11 cm (4¹/4 in) and 16 rows to 10 cm (4 in) measured over mesh pattern using 2.00 mm hook. Change hook size if necessary to obtain this tension.

ABBREVIATIONS

dc2tog – *insert hook as indicated, yoh and draw loop through, rep from * once more, yoh and draw through all 3 loops on hook; **tr2tog** – *yoh and insert hook as indicated, yoh and draw loop through, yoh and draw through 2 loops, rep from * once more, yoh and draw through all 3 loops on hook; **tr3tog** – *yoh and insert hook as indicated, yoh and draw loop through, yoh and draw through 2 loops, rep from * twice more, yoh and draw through all 4 loops on hook.

See also page 15.

For how to work with beads, see pages 16–17.

BODICE

With 2.00 mm hook, make 260 (276: 292: 308: 324: 340) ch and join with a ss to form a ring.

Foundation round: (RS) 3 ch (counts as first tr), miss ch at base of 3 ch, 1 tr into each ch to end, ss to top of 3 ch at beg of round, turn. 260 (276: 292: 308: 324: 340) sts.

Cont in tr fabric as follows:

Round 1: (WS) 3 ch (counts as 1 tr), miss st at base of 3 ch, 1 tr into each tr to end, ss to top of 3 ch at beg of round, turn.

- Twilleys Silky is a very slippery yarn and the stitches can easily fall undone. Each time you put your work down, it's a good idea to slip the working loop onto a safety pin to make sure it does not unravel!
- You could make this dress longer or shorter by simply working more or less rows in the skirt section. But remember this will mean the amount of yarn you need will change!

- As the dress will "drop" slightly in wear, it's a good idea to measure the length of the skirt section with it hanging, not laid flat.
- Remember to thread the tie through the underbust casing before working the second tassel end as the beads will be difficult to thread through the crochet.
- Teardrop pearl beads come in two sorts – those that have their threading hole across the top narrow end, and those that are drilled from top to bottom. Make sure you buy the sort with the hole at the top!

This round forms tr fabric. (Beg and end of rounds is centre back point.)
Work a further 10 rounds in tr fabric, ending with a WS round.
Fasten off.

Shape top edge

Miss first 73 (79: 85: 91: 97: 103) sts of next round, rejoin yarn to next tr with RS facing, 3 ch (counts as first tr), miss tr where yarn was rejoined, 1 tr into each of next 52 (54: 56: 58: 60: 62) tr, tr3tog over next 3 tr, 1 tr into next tr (this is tr before centre front point) and turn, leaving rem sts unworked.
Work in tr fabric in **rows** on this set of 55 (57: 59: 61: 63: 65) sts only for first side of top edge.
Next row: 3 ch (counts as first tr), tr3tog over next 3 sts – 2 sts decreased, 1 tr into each tr to last 4 sts, tr3tog over next 3 sts – 2 sts decreased, 1 tr into top of 3 ch at beg of previous row, turn. 51 (53: 55: 57: 59: 61) sts.
Working all decreases as set by last row, dec 2 sts at each end of next 8 (10: 6: 8: 4: 6) rows, ending with a WS row. 19 (13: 31: 25: 43: 37) sts.
Next row: (RS) 3 ch (counts as first tr), tr2tog over next 2 sts – 1 st decreased, 1 tr into each tr to last 4 sts, tr3tog over next 3 sts – 2 sts decreased, 1 tr into top of 3 ch at beg of previous row, turn.
Next row: 3 ch (counts as first tr), tr3tog over next 3 sts – 2 sts decreased, 1 tr into each tr to last 3 sts, tr2tog over next 2 sts – 1 st decreased, 1 tr into top of 3 ch at beg of

previous row, turn. 13 (7: 25: 19: 37: 31) sts.
Rep last 2 rows 1 (0: 3: 2: 5: 4) times more, then first of these rows again. 4 sts.
Next row: (WS) 3 ch (does NOT count as st), tr3tog over last 3 sts.
Fasten off.
Return to last complete round worked, with RS facing rejoin yarn to next tr after first side of top edge, 3 ch (counts as first tr), miss tr where yarn was rejoined, tr3tog over next 3 tr, 1 tr into each of next 53 (55: 57: 59: 61: 63) tr and turn, leaving rem sts unworked. 55 (57: 59: 61: 63: 65) sts.
Working all shaping as set by first side, dec 2 sts at centre front edge of next 14 (14: 16: 16: 18: 18) rows and at the same time dec 2 sts at side edge of next 9 (11: 7: 9: 5: 7) rows, then 1 st at this edge on foll 5 (3: 9: 7: 13: 11) rows. 4 sts.
Next row: (WS) 3 ch (does NOT count as st), tr3tog over last 3 sts.
Fasten off.

SKIRT

With RS facing and using 2.00 mm hook, rejoin yarn to foundation ch edge of Bodice at centre back, 1 ch (does NOT count as st), 1 dc into each foundation ch, ss to first dc, turn. 260 (276: 292: 308: 324: 340) sts.
Round 2: (WS) 1 ch (does NOT count as st), 1 dc into each dc to end, ss to first dc, turn.
Round 3: 4 ch (counts as first tr and 1 ch), miss dc at base of 4 ch and next dc, *1 tr into next dc, 1 ch, miss 1 dc, rep from * to end, ss to 3rd

KEY

⬯ ch
+ dc

⊤ tr

of 4 ch at beg of round, turn.

Round 4: 1 ch (does NOT count as st), 1 dc into each ch sp and tr to end, ss to first dc, turn.

Round 5: As round 2.

These 5 rounds complete underbust section.

Next round: (WS) 1 ch (does NOT count as st), 1 dc into first dc, [5 ch, miss 3 dc, 1 dc into next dc] 8 (7: 8: 8: 9: 8) times, [5 ch, miss 2 dc, 1 dc into next dc] 22 (26: 26: 30: 30: 34) times, [5 ch, miss 3 dc, 1 dc into next dc] 16 (16: 18: 16: 18: 18) times, [5 ch, miss 2 dc, 1 dc into next dc] 22 (26: 26: 30: 30: 34) times, [5 ch, miss 3 dc, 1 dc into next dc] 7 (6: 7: 7: 8: 7) times, 5 ch, miss 3 dc, ss to dc at beg of round, turn. 76 (82: 86: 92: 96: 102) ch sps.

Cont in mesh patt as follows:

Round 1: (RS) 3 ch (counts as first tr), 2 tr into dc at base of 3 ch, *1 dc into next ch sp, 5 ch, miss 1 dc, 1 dc into next ch sp**, 5 tr into next dc, rep from * to end, ending last rep at **, 2 tr into same place as tr at beg of round, ss to top of 3 ch at beg of round. 38 (41: 43: 46: 48: 51) patt reps.

Round 2: 1 ch (does NOT count as st), 1 dc into same place as ss at end of previous round, *5 ch, miss (2 tr and 1 dc), 1 dc into next ch sp**, 5 ch, miss (1 dc and 2 tr), 1 dc into next tr, rep from * to end, ending last rep at **, 2 ch, miss (1 dc and 2 tr), 1 tr into dc at beg of round.

Round 3: 1 ch (does NOT count as st), 1 dc into ch sp partly formed by tr at end of previous round, *5 ch, miss 1 dc, 1 dc into next ch sp, 5 tr into next dc, 1 dc into next ch sp, rep from * to end, replacing dc at end of last rep with ss to first dc.

Round 4: ss across and into centre of first ch sp, 1 ch (does NOT count as st), 1 dc into same ch sp, *5 ch, miss (1 dc and 2 tr), 1 dc into next tr, 5 ch, miss (2 tr and 1 dc), 1 dc into next ch sp, rep from * to end, replacing dc at end of last rep with ss to first dc.

These 4 rounds form mesh patt.

Cont in mesh patt until Skirt measures 62 (63: 63: 64: 64: 65) cm, 24$\frac{1}{2}$ (24$\frac{3}{4}$: 24$\frac{3}{4}$: 25: 25: 25$\frac{1}{2}$) ins, from round 5 of underbust section, ending with patt round 2 or 4. 76 (82: 86: 92: 96: 102) ch sps. Fasten off.

Work hem border

Thread beads onto yarn.

With RS facing, rejoin yarn into one ch sp at centre back and cont as follows:

Round 1: 1 ch (does NOT count as st), 1 dc into ch sp where yarn was rejoined, *7 ch, (1 dc, 1 beaded ch and 1 dc) into next ch sp, rep from * to end, replacing dc at end of last rep with ss to first dc.

Round 2: ss along and into centre of first ch sp, 1 ch (does NOT count as st), 1 dc into same ch sp, *9 ch, (1 dc, 1 beaded ch and 1 dc) into next ch sp, rep from * to end, replacing dc at end of last rep with ss to first dc.

Round 3: ss along and into centre of first ch sp, 1 ch (does NOT count as st), 1 dc into same ch sp, *6 ch, 1 beaded ch, miss beaded ch, ss to next ch, 5 ch, (1 dc, 1 beaded ch and 1 dc) into next ch sp, rep from * to end, replacing dc at end of last rep with ss to first dc.

Fasten off.

TO MAKE UP
Do NOT press.

Front Neck Edging
With RS facing and using 2.00 mm hook, rejoin yarn at fasten-off point at top of left front edge, 1 ch (does NOT count as st), work one row of dc evenly down left front slope, then up right front slope to other fasten-off point, turn.
Next row: (WS) 1 ch (does NOT count as st), 1 dc into each dc to end, working dc2tog at either side of base of centre front V neck, turn.
Rep last row once more.
Do NOT fasten off.

Armhole and Back Edging and Shoulder Straps
With RS facing and using 2.00 mm hook, attach separate length of yarn to beg of last row of Front Neck Edging, make 94 (94: 96: 96: 98: 98) ch (for left shoulder strap) and fasten off.
With RS facing, using 2.00 mm hook and yarn left at end of Front Neck Edging, make 95 (95: 97: 97: 99: 99) ch (for right shoulder strap), 1 dc into 2nd ch from hook, 1 dc into each of next 93 (93: 95: 95: 97: 97) ch, work one row of dc evenly down right armhole edge, across back, then up left armhole edge to ch at top of Front Neck Edging, 1 dc into each ch to end, turn.
Next row: (WS) 1 ch (does NOT count as st), 1 dc into each dc to end, missing dc as required to ensure edging lies flat, turn.
Rep last row once more. Fasten off.

Underbust Tie
Threads 6 beads onto yarn.
Using 2.00 mm hook, make a ch approx 140 (145: 150: 155: 160: 165) cm long and cont as follows: 22 ch, 1 beaded ch, miss beaded ch, 1 dc into each of next 22 ch, 1 ss into next ch, 29 ch, 1 beaded ch, miss beaded ch, 1 dc into each

of next 29 ch, 1 ss into same ch as already worked into for first strand of tassel, 16 ch, 1 beaded ch, miss beaded ch, 1 dc into each of next 16 ch, 1 ss into is same ch as already worked into for first and second strands of tassel, 1 dc into each ch to end, break off yarn leaving a very long end but do NOT fasten off. Leave working loop on a safety pin.
Starting and ending at centre front, thread Tie in and out of round 3 of underbust section. Insert hook into working loop and complete tassel at other end of Tie as follows: 22 ch, 1 beaded ch, miss beaded ch, 1 dc into each of next 22 ch, 1 ss into is same ch as last dc was worked into before Tie was threaded through, 29 ch, 1 beaded ch, miss beaded ch, 1 dc into each of next 29 ch, 1 ss into same ch as already worked into for first strand of tassel, 16 ch, 1 beaded ch, miss beaded ch, 1 dc into each of next 16 ch, 1 ss into is same ch as already worked into for first and second strands of tassel.
Fasten off.
Try on dress and adjust length of shoulder straps, attaching them to inside of back edging.

Index